I0796295

NORTH AMERICAN FIELD GUIDES

MUSHROOMS AND OTHER FUNGI

Mari Bolte

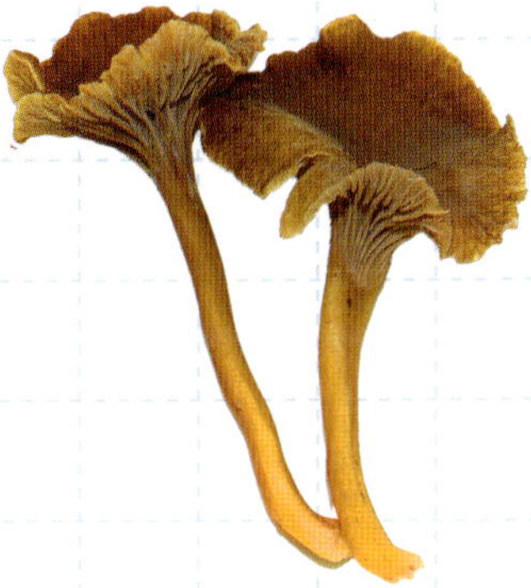

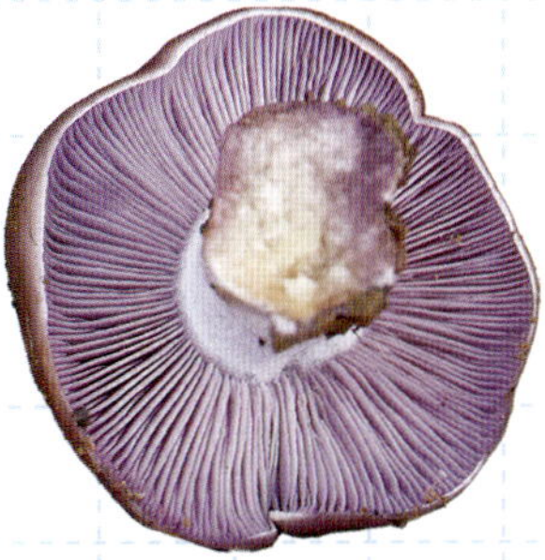

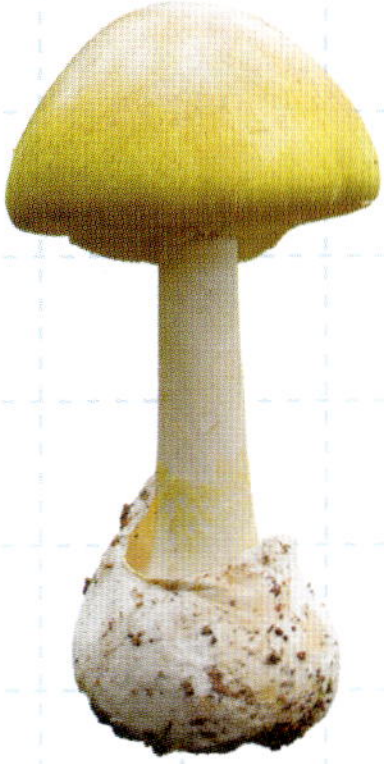

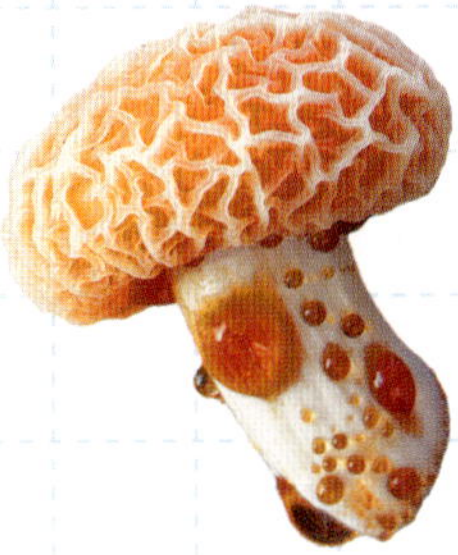

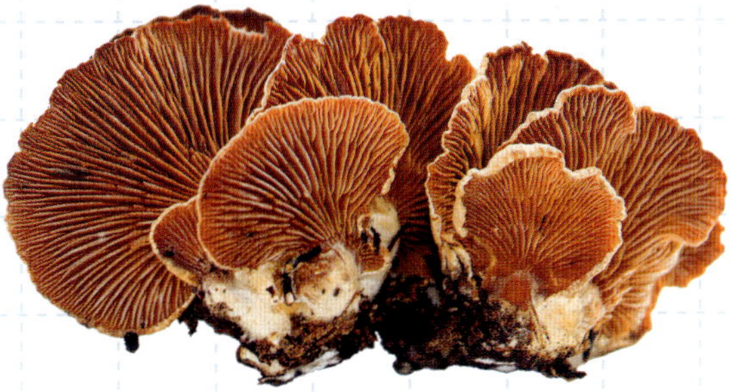

An Imprint of Abdo Reference | abdobooks.com

CONTENTS

What Are Fungi?....................4
How to Use This Book....................6

Mycorrhizal Mushrooms

American Slender Caesar....................8
Amethyst Deceiver....................9
Black Trumpet....................10
Bleeding Tooth....................11
Chanterelle....................12
Deadly Webcap....................13
Death Cap....................14
Deer Truffle....................15
Destroying Angel....................16
Dyeball Fungus....................17
Fly Amanita....................18
Green-Spored Lepiota....................19
Hedgehog....................20
Indigo Milky Cap....................21
Matsutake....................22
Oregon Black Truffle....................23
Panther Cap....................24
Saffron Milky Cap....................25
Slippery Jack....................26
Weeping Milkcap....................27
Woolly Milkcap....................28
Yellowfoot....................29

Parasitic Mushrooms

Cauliflower....................30
Dyer's Polypore....................31
Hen-of-the-Woods....................32
Honey....................33
Lion's Mane....................34
Lobster....................35
Reishi....................36
Witch's Butter....................37

Saprotrophic Mushrooms

Angel Wing....................38
Apricot Jelly....................39
Artist's Conk....................40
Beefsteak....................41
Bird's Nest....................42
Bitter Oyster....................43
Blewit....................44
Brain Puffball....................45
Brick Cap....................46
Chicken of the Woods....................47
Collared Earthstar....................48
Comb Tooth....................49
Common Brown Cup....................50
Common Conecap....................51
Common Puffball....................52
Common Stinkhorn....................53
Crown-Tipped Coral....................54
Dead Man's Finger....................55
Death Angel....................56
Devil's Cigar....................57
Dryad's Saddle....................58
Dung Cannon....................59
Elfin Saddle....................60
Eyelash Cup....................61
False Morel....................62
Fluted Bird's Nest....................63
Giant Puffball....................64
Jack-o-Lantern....................65
Little Ping Pong Bat....................66
Mica Cap....................67
Morel....................68

Oak Mazegill 69
Octopus Stinkhorn 70
Orange Peel 71
Oyster 72
Parasol 73
Porcini 74
Portobello 75
Prince Agaricus 76
Purple Jellydisc 77
Red Basket Stinkhorn 78
Red Belted Conk 79
Scarlet Elf Cup 80
Shaggy Mane 81
Shaggy Parasol 82
Shiitake 83
Splitgill 84
Straw 85
Sun 86
Turkey Tail 87
Veiled Lady Stinkhorn 88
Violet-Toothed Polypore 89
Vomiting Russula 90
Weeping Willow 91
Wood Ear 92
Wrinkled Peach 93

Lichens

Devil's Matchstick 94
Old Man's Beard 95
Reindeer Moss 96
Trumpet Cup 97
Witch's Hair 98
Wolf Lichen 99

Smuts

Corn Smut 100
Stinking Smut 101

Other Fungi

Black Stem Rust 102
Ergot 103
Hollyhock Rust 104
Scarlet Caterpillarclub 105
White Pine Blister Rust 106
Zombie-Ant Fungus 107

Glossary 108
To Learn More 109
Photo Credits 110

WHAT ARE FUNGI?

Fungi come in five forms: mushrooms, yeast, mold, lichens, and mildew. Mushrooms are fungi's fruit. These umbrella-, cup-, or ear-shaped organs are also called sporophores. They spread spores and allow the fungi to reproduce. They come in many shapes, sizes, and colors. Some are even invisible to the human eye.

Mushrooms and fungi are not plants or animals. For many years, scientists thought they were a plant. Then, they discovered that mushrooms and fungi are more like animals because they do not make their own food through photosynthesis as plants do. Instead, they absorb nutrients from other organic things, living or dead. Mushrooms also do not have leaves, roots, or seeds. They reproduce either sexually or asexually.

Mushrooms and fungi are connected through a network of thin, root-like filaments called hyphae. The hyphae wind together into a larger mass called a mycelium. It usually grows underground but can also thrive in damp places such as rotting wood. Most mycelia can be too small to see, but some stretch for acres. A branching hypha can grow as much as half a mile (0.8 km) a day. The largest mycelium in the world belongs to a honey mushroom in eastern Oregon. It stretches across 2,200 acres (890 ha) and has been estimated to be between 2,000 and 8,000 years old.

WHAT DO MUSHROOMS LOOK LIKE?

There are about 45,000 known mushroom and fungi species in North America, and as many as 5.1 million around the world. However, only about 120,000 have been named. Most of them are microscopic, so they can't be seen with the human eye. Mushrooms that are visible to the human eye are divided into three categories: mycorrhizal, saprotrophic, and parasitic.

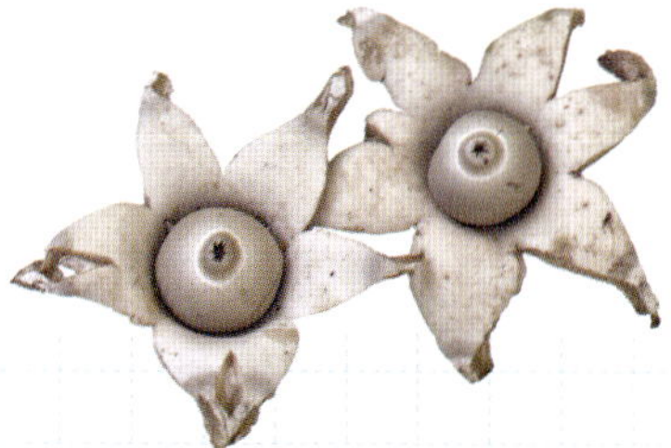

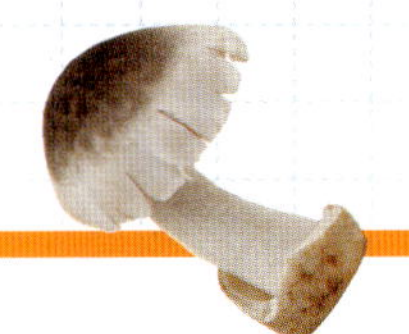

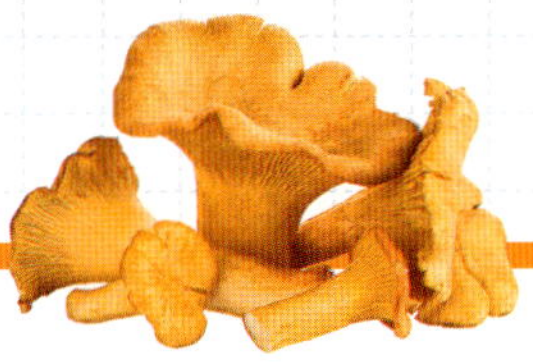

Mycorrhizal mushrooms form a symbiotic relationship with plant and tree roots. The mushroom's mycelia wrap around the tree's roots, helping the tree absorb more water and nutrients. The mushrooms also filter out toxic materials, such as pesticides or impurities in water. In turn, the tree gives the mushroom some of the sugars it makes during photosynthesis. More than 90 percent of plants in an ecosystem rely on symbiotic mushrooms.

Saprotrophic mushrooms decompose dead organic matter and absorb those nutrients. Dead wood, plants, and even animals can be broken down by saprotrophic mushrooms. The word *saprotrophic* comes from the Greek words for "rotten" (*saprops*) and "food" (*trophe*).

Parasitic mushrooms attach themselves to plants and trees like mycorrhizals. However, they break down living organic matter, harming rather than helping the host.

WHAT ROLE DO MUSHROOMS PLAY?

Mushrooms are identified by their shape, cap, stem, spore-bearing area, veils, and odor. Additional details, such as size, color, texture, and location, are also used. Taking spore prints can help distinguish two similar species. There are edible species, but some can cause sickness. Mushrooms can also absorb chemicals from their environment—such as pesticides or fertilizers. Use caution while mushroom hunting.

SPORE PRINTS

To take a spore print, cut off the mushroom's stem. Set the cap gill-side-down on a flat surface. Moisten the cap with a drop of water, and then cover with a glass. In 2 to 24 hours, the cap will drop its spores. Carefully lift the cap to examine the print.

HOW TO USE THIS BOOK

Tab shows the fungus's category.

The fungus's common name appears here.

MYCORRHIZAL MUSHROOMS

BLACK TRUMPET

(CRATERELLUS CORNUCOPIOIDES)

Black trumpets are believed to be both mycorrhizal and saprotrophic, growing near host trees and breaking down organic matter on the forest floor. Its dark color and small size ake it difficult to find. They typically grow in large, ti htly packed bunches on the ground in the summer and fall and grow back in the same places year after year. The mushrooms are tight at the base and flare near the top, ... shroom its name.

This paragraph gives information about the fungus.

HOW TO SPOT

Size: 1.2 to 2 inches (3 to 5 cm) wide; 2 to 3.5 inches (5 to 8.9 cm) tall

Color: Dark gray to black

Habitat: Deciduous and coniferous forests

Range: East of the Rocky Mountains, along the West Coast

WHAT'S ITS NAME?

Some experts believe that black trumpet mushrooms have a European species and a North American species. They are genetically identical, with the only difference being that the European form, *C. cornucopioides*, has a white spore print, and the print of North America's *C. fallax* is more salmon in color. However, *C. cornucopioides* is ... d to refer to both species.

10

Sidebars provide additional information about the topic.

The fungus's scientific name appears here.

EEDING TOOTH *(HYDNELLUM PECKII)*

ɛe its creepy appearance, the bleeding tooth
ɾoom—also known as the devil's tooth—is not
ɘrous. It is a hydnoid fungi, which can be identified
e tooth-like spines underneath the cap. The spines,
ı are the fungus's reproductive organs, grow spores
are released into the air. Pockets filled with sticky red
ɟ are believed to keep animals and insects away. As the
ıroom ages, the cap shrinks and the liquid dries up.

Fun Facts give interesting information about the fungus.

FUN FACT

Another common name for this mushroom is strawberries and cream. But this mushroom has a bitter taste and an unpleasant smell.

How to Spot features give information about the fungus's size, color, habitat, and North American range.

HOW TO SPOT

Size: 1 to 4 inches (2.5 to 10.2 cm) wide
Color: Pink or white, with droplets of red sap across the top
Habitat: Deciduous and coniferous forests
Range: Throughout North America

Images show the fungus.

11

AMERICAN SLENDER CAESAR

(AMANITA JACKSONII)

The American slender Caesar has a bright red cap and yellow-orange stem. These mushrooms begin inside egg-like capsules. The stem lengthens and the cup expands, leaving the volva behind. Gills are closely spaced and pale yellow. As the mushroom ages, the red cap lightens, and striations along the edges become visible. This variety is edible, with a soft, chewy texture and cheesy flavor. However, because it is so similar to other toxic *Amanitas*, it should be picked with caution.

HOW TO SPOT

Size: 3 to 6 inches (7.6 to 15.2 cm) wide; 3 to 8 inches (7.6 to 20.3 cm) tall

Color: Red cap that fades along the edges as the mushroom ages

Habitat: Deciduous and coniferous forests

Range: Eastern North America, from Canada to Mexico

FUN FACT

There are between 900 and 1,000 known members of the *Amanita* genus around the world. Some are edible, but ingesting just a small amount of a toxic species can lead to death or serious illness.

AMETHYST DECEIVER

(LACCARIA AMETHYSTINA)

With curved, bright purple caps, the amethyst deceiver is easy to spot when young. As it ages, the cap fades to lilac, tan, or brown, and it flattens out. Its gills are thick and waxy. The gills are attached to the long, thin stem and match the cap in color. Stems are fibrous and tough, with hair-like fuzz closer to the base. This mushroom is easy to find when it grows in moss, but it is harder to find in dark leaf litter until it ages and lightens in color.

HOW TO SPOT

Size: 0.2 to 1.4 inches (0.5 to 3.6 cm) wide; 0.4 to 2.8 inches (1 to 7.1 cm) tall

Color: Bright purple, fading with age

Habitat: Deciduous and coniferous forests

Range: Forests east of the Rocky Mountains

LOOK-ALIKES

Of the approximately 14,000 known mushroom species around the world, only 2,200 of them are considered edible. Fewer than 100 are toxic, and only one to two dozen of those are lethal to humans. However, many of them look similar to edible varieties. When gathering wild mushrooms, be sure of the species!

BLACK TRUMPET

(CRATERELLUS CORNUCOPIOIDES)

Black trumpets are believed to be both mycorrhizal and saprotrophic, growing near host trees and breaking down organic matter on the forest floor. Its dark color and small size make it difficult to find. They typically grow in large, tightly packed bunches on the ground in the summer and fall and grow back in the same places year after year. The mushrooms are tight at the base and flare near the top, giving the mushroom its name.

HOW TO SPOT

Size: 1.2 to 2 inches (3 to 5 cm) wide; 2 to 3.5 inches (5 to 8.9 cm) tall

Color: Dark gray to black

Habitat: Deciduous and coniferous forests

Range: East of the Rocky Mountains, along the West Coast

WHAT'S ITS NAME?

Some experts believe that black trumpet mushrooms have a European species and a North American species. They are genetically identical, with the only difference being that the European form, *C. cornucopioides*, has a white spore print, and the print of North America's *C. fallax* is more salmon in color. However, *C. cornucopioides* is commonly used to refer to both species.

BLEEDING TOOTH *(HYDNELLUM PECKII)*

Despite its creepy appearance, the bleeding tooth mushroom—also known as the devil's tooth—is not dangerous. It is a hydnoid fungi, which can be identified by the tooth-like spines underneath the cap. The spines, which are the fungus's reproductive organs, grow spores that are released into the air. Pockets filled with sticky red liquid are believed to keep animals and insects away. As the mushroom ages, the cap shrinks and the liquid dries up.

FUN FACT

Another common name for this mushroom is strawberries and cream. But this mushroom has a bitter taste and an unpleasant smell.

HOW TO SPOT

Size: 1 to 4 inches (2.5 to 10.2 cm) wide

Color: Pink or white, with droplets of red sap across the top

Habitat: Deciduous and coniferous forests

Range: Throughout North America

CHANTERELLE

(CANTHARELLUS CIBARIUS)

With their golden caps, chanterelles are easy to spot in wooded areas in the summer and fall. They are known for their fruity, apricot-like odor. Chanterelles do not have gills like most mushrooms. Instead, they have false gills, or pseudo-gills, that do not move or detach from the cap or stem. Chanterelles prefer moist ground and humid conditions. Clusters can be found several days after heavy rains. Although they have a limited growing season, they appear in the same place year after year.

HOW TO SPOT

Size: 1 to 4 inches (2.5 to 10 cm) wide; 2 to 4 inches (5 to 10.2 cm) tall

Color: Bright shades of yellow, gold, and orange

Habitat: Deciduous and coniferous forests

Range: Throughout North America

Chanterelle

False Chanterelle

FAKERS

The chanterelle has a look-alike species, called the false chanterelle. However, unlike its namesake, the false chanterelle is saprotrophic. Other differences include deeper, forked orange gills that move when touched and a color difference. False chanterelles are more orange, both outside and inside the stem. They have a more rounded shape, and the stem has a consistent thickness from top to bottom.

DEADLY WEBCAP

(CORTINARIUS RUBELLUS)

The deadly webcap is easily confused with chanterelles. It has an earthy smell and loves damp, acidic soil and mossy ground near pine or spruce trees. Unlike chanterelles, deadly webcaps have true gills that are pale yellow or brown. The curved stem is lighter than the cap, and the cap comes in a variety of shapes, from conical to flat. Every part of the mushroom is toxic. Even a small piece of deadly webcap can cause serious health issues.

HOW TO SPOT

Size: 1 to 3.1 inches (2.5 to 7.9 cm) wide; 2 to 4.3 inches (5 to 10.9 cm) tall
Color: Brown or orange
Habitat: Coniferous forests
Range: Northern and western North America

FUN FACT

Deadly webcaps contain a poison called orellanine. At first, victims feel as though they have the common flu, but real symptoms can show up two days to as long as three weeks later. It can cause kidney failure or even death.

DEATH CAP *(AMANITA PHALLOIDES)*

Death cap mushrooms are not native to North America. They were imported with plants coming from Europe. They spread and became an invasive species. They are one of the most fatal mushrooms in the world, and only a small amount of the cap can kill. Most people who die of mushroom poisoning ate death cap. The domed white cap resembles many types of edible mushrooms, although older death caps smell rancid as their caps flatten and mature. The stalk is off-white and wider at the base, sitting in a volva.

HOW TO SPOT

Size: 1.6 to 6.3 inches (4.1 to 16 cm) wide; 6 inches (15.2 cm) tall

Color: White or off-white

Habitat: Deciduous forests

Range: West Coast of North America; as far east as Idaho

DEER TRUFFLE

(ELAPHOMYCES GRANULATUS)

Deer truffles are hypogeous, which means they live and grow beneath the earth's surface. Deer truffles grow in cool, moist habitats all year long. The outside of the fruiting body is tough and bark-like. The inside is full of spores. When the fruit is young, the spores are solid and light gray. By the time they are ready to be released, they are a dark, loose powder. Despite their name, deer truffles are not considered edible by humans since they are tough and do not taste good.

HOW TO SPOT

Size: 2 inches (5 cm) in diameter
Color: Light brown outside
Habitat: Coniferous forests
Range: Canada and the United States

FINDERS KEEPERS

Because they live underground, deer truffles are hard to locate. Sometimes parasitic fungi attach themselves to deer truffles. The fungus's fruiting body appears aboveground, clueing in foragers to the truffle's presence. Wild animals, such as deer or wild boars, can sniff out deer truffles too.

DESTROYING ANGEL

(AMANITA BISPORIGERA)

Easy to spot with its smooth, bald white cap, the destroying angel, also known as the death angel, can be found near the ground in hardwood forests. Its white cap turns tan in the center as it ages. Its gills are close-set and not attached to the long, soft, curved stem. The annulus is near the cap, and the mushroom rests on a white volva. Eating a destroying angel can be severe, or even deadly. Its main toxin, alpha-amanitin, attacks the liver and causes it to fail.

HOW TO SPOT

Size: 4 inches (10.2 cm) wide
Color: White
Habitat: Deciduous forests
Range: Eastern North America, from Canada to Mexico

DYEBALL FUNGUS

(PISOLITHUS ARHIZUS)

In Greek, this mushroom's scientific name means "rootless pea-stone." However, its more common nicknames are dog turd fungus and dead man's foot. This hardy fungus can grow in places many other fungi cannot. Dyeball fungus can survive near hot geysers and in sand; it can even grow through asphalt. It can form mycorrhizal relationships with most plant types and tree roots. The fungus's fruiting body contains spores, which are released when the fruit splits.

FUN FACT

Dyeballs are used to naturally color wool. The insides are full of gelatinous liquid that turns the wool black or brown.

HOW TO SPOT

Size: Up to 8 inches (20.3 cm) wide

Color: Dull brown

Habitat: Deciduous and coniferous forests

Range: Across North America

FLY AMANITA *(AMANITA MUSCARIA)*

Also known as the fly agaric, the fly amanita is large and easy to spot near birch, pine, and spruce trees. Young mushrooms are covered with a thin layer of tissue. As the mushroom grows, the tissue tears, becoming the white spots that decorate the cap. White gills are close to each other and only attach to the cap's underside. There may be a thin annulus. The stalk below is covered in ringed scales. Fly amanita are not edible.

HOW TO SPOT

Size: Up to 7.9 inches (20 cm) wide and 11.8 inches (30 cm) tall

Color: Red with white spots

Habitat: Deciduous and coniferous forests

Range: Eastern North America, from Canada to Tennessee

GREEN-SPORED LEPIOTA

(CHLOROPHYLLUM MOLYBDITES)

The green-spored lepiota is also known as the false parasol. It grows in grassy areas in the summer and fall, often in a fairy ring, giving it the additional nickname of the "backyard mushroom." The thick, closely spaced gills are greenish, which distinguishes this mushroom from other parasol varieties. The stalk is wider at the base, with a partial veil. Green-spored lepiota are toxic and can cause stomach upset. In the United States, it is the most common cause of mushroom poisoning.

Size: 2 to 12 inches (5 to 30.5 cm) wide; 3 to 10 inches (7.6 to 25.4 cm) tall

Color: White with large, cream or brown scales on the cap

Habitat: Deciduous and coniferous forests; flat, grassy areas

Range: Across North America

FUN FACT

Fairy rings occur when mushrooms grow in a circle. Some folktales say they are created by elves, fairies, witches, or dragons. Others believe they are portals to fantasy worlds.

HEDGEHOG *(HYDNUM REPANDUM)*

The hedgehog mushroom is an edible fungus. In France, it is known as *Pied de Mouton*, or sheep's foot. They have a distinct look, with large, soft caps that curve along the top and turn up around the edges. The flesh is firm and velvety. Instead of gills, the underside is covered in soft, spiny teeth. Although it is not edible raw, it is delicious when cooked and there are no toxic look-alike species, which makes it an ideal mushroom for beginner foragers.

HOW TO SPOT

Size: 2.4 to 6 inches (6 to 15.2 cm) wide; 1.2 to 2.4 inches (3 to 6 cm) tall

Color: Creamy white or pale buff

Habitat: Deciduous and coniferous forests

Range: Across North America

INDIGO MILKY CAP *(LACTARIUS INDIGO)*

Indigo milky caps are edible and beautiful. They get their name from the dark blue milky liquid that oozes out when the mushroom is cut. Young indigo milky caps are sticky and have a cap that curves slightly inward and unfurls as the mushroom ages. Cut edges of the mushroom will eventually turn green when exposed to air. The gills attach to the stem and are deep blue to gray. The chemical that makes the indigo milky cap has been used as a natural fabric dye.

FUN FACT

As long as they have received enough rain, all *Lacterius* species of mushroom ooze liquid when cut. Many milky caps are not edible due to the bitter taste. However, the indigo milky cap is not one of those.

HOW TO SPOT

Size: 2 to 6 inches (5 to 15.2 cm) wide; 0.8 to 3.1 inches (2 to 7.9 cm) tall

Color: Faded blue

Habitat: Deciduous and coniferous forests

Range: Across North America

MATSUTAKE *(TRICHOLOMA MAGNIVELARE)*

In the fall, mushroom hunters use their noses to find *T. magnivelare*. It has a strong scent of cinnamon, spice, and citrus. It is found on the ground beneath hard pines, such as red, pitch, or jack. Needles from the tree hide and protect the mushrooms. Young matsutakes start with cap edges that roll in and a veil that protects the gills. As the mushroom ages, the cap flattens, exposing the white gills underneath and revealing brown, fibrous scales starting in its center. The stem is thick and covered with scales as well.

HOW TO SPOT

Size: 1.6 to 3.5 inches (4 to 8.9 cm) wide; 1.6 to 4 inches (4 to 10.2 cm) tall

Color: White and light brown

Habitat: Coniferous forests

Range: Northern North America, stretching south through the Appalachian Mountains

FUN FACT

There are three types of matsutake mushrooms in North America. However, the most famous in this family, *T. matsutake*, is found in East Asia and northern Europe.

OREGON BLACK TRUFFLE

(LEUCANGIUM CARTHUSIANUM)

Lacking a stem, cap, or gills, truffles look more like potatoes than mushrooms. Although the famous truffles grown in France or Italy are not native to North America, their cousin, *L. carthusianum*, is. Found in damp, fern-covered forests, Oregon black truffles are most often found near Douglas fir trees. Young truffles have a scent similar to tropical fruit. This later develops into a deeper odor resembling chocolate or cheese. Sharp-nosed animals such as dogs and hogs can sniff out ripe truffles, but the scent only lasts about a week.

FUN FACT

Because Oregon black truffles live underground, they depend on animals to dig them up and eat them. Their spores are spread through the animals' feces.

HOW TO SPOT

Size: 1 to 5 inches (2.5 to 12.7 cm) wide
Color: Black on the outside, marbled gray and white on the inside
Habitat: Coniferous forests
Range: Northwest North America

PANTHER CAP *(AMANITA PANTHERINA)*

Getting its name from its mottled cap, the panther cap mushroom is beautiful and deadly. Young panther caps are rounded, with the edges close to the thick stem. As it ages, the cap unfurls, leaving tissue behind on the stem and revealing tightly packed gills. Panther caps are not native to North America. It is believed that trees imported from Europe carried the spores with them. It has adapted to live in urban areas, which puts dogs and young children at higher risk of accidentally consuming them.

HOW TO SPOT

Size: 2 to 4 inches (5 to 10.2 cm) wide; 1.6 to 7.9 inches (4 to 20 cm) tall

Color: Brown with white spots

Habitat: Deciduous and coniferous forests

Range: Pacific Northwest

FUN FACT

When consumed, the panther cap's psychoactive ingredients can cause symptoms as mild as a dreamy, out-of-body experience or as major as fainting, amnesia, or seizures.

SAFFRON MILKY CAP

(LACTARIUS DELICIOSUS)

Both its common and scientific names describe this orange-colored mushroom that's full of milky orange goo. The latex-like liquid is released from the milky cap's spores, turning green when exposed to the air. The caps are mottled with orange rings and are easy to spot in the late fall to early winter. The thick stem is hollow. Some people find *L. deliciosus* lives up to its name, although it must be cooked a long time or it can be grainy or bitter.

HOW TO SPOT

Size: 2 to 5.9 inches (5 to 15 cm) wide; 1.2 to 2.4 inches (3 to 6 cm) tall

Color: Orange

Habitat: Coniferous forests

Range: Western North America

FUN FACT

There are several varieties of *L. deliciosus* across North America. Scientists are still working on categorizing variant subspecies.

SLIPPERY JACK *(SUILLUS LUTEUS)*

A convex brown cap that looks and feels sticky gives this mushroom another nickname—the sticky bun. It has thrived in pine forests where it is both foraged for and grown intentionally. It can be found in the late summer and fall, and even into winter if the climate is warm enough. The cap is flat or convex, with a spongy layer underneath instead of gills. An annulus is visible around the stalk, which is slimy as well. Slippery jack must be peeled, as eating the slimy skin can cause stomach upset.

HOW TO SPOT

Size: 1.6 to 4 inches (4 to 10.2 cm) wide; 1.2 to 3.1 inches (3 to 7.9 cm) tall
Color: Shiny brown
Habitat: Coniferous forests
Range: Across North America

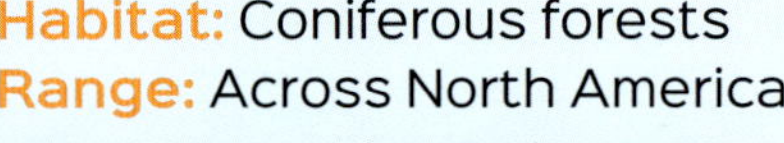

FUN FACT

There are around 100 *Suillus* species around the world. *S. luteus* is the most widespread.

WEEPING MILKCAP

(LACTIFLUUS VOLEMUS)

This fishy-smelling fungus grows out of the ground. It has a thick, squat stalk and an apricot color. The smooth cap is slightly convex with an edge that rolls under when young and flattens out with age. It is velvety to the touch. Gills are lighter, with both long and short gills. When damaged, the gills discolor and leak milky latex that starts white and then turns a brown color that stains. As the mushroom dries, the dead fish smell becomes even more pungent. The smell disappears when the mushroom is cooked.

HOW TO SPOT

Size: 1 to 5 inches (2.5 to 12.7 cm) wide; 2 to 4 inches (5 to 10.2 cm) tall

Color: Orange to light brown

Habitat: Deciduous and coniferous forests

Range: Across North America

WOOLLY MILKCAP

(LACTARIUS TORMINOSUS)

Salmon pink on the outside and creamy white on the inside, the woolly milkcap has a shaggy cap covering and a white, milky latex that is released when the narrow gills are damaged. It can be found near birch trees by the edge of wooded areas. The cap is convex or even fluted, with pinkish-orange bands of color. Its thick stem is pale orange or buff. Some value the mushroom for its spicy flavor, but many others consider it poisonous. When eaten raw, the mushroom can cause blisters in the mouth and an upset stomach.

HOW TO SPOT

Size: 1.6 to 4.7 inches (4 to 11.9 cm) wide; 1.2 to 3.1 inches (3 to 7.9 cm) tall

Color: White with light brown or orange rings

Habitat: Deciduous forests

Range: Across North America

FUN FACT

More than 200 types of milkcaps have been documented in North America.

YELLOWFOOT

(CRATERELLUS TUBAEFORMIS)

Yellowfoot is a small member of the chanterelle family. They can be found during early winter until the ground completely freezes. They have a fruity smell, delicate flavor, and firm texture. The caps are brown, and the wrinkled false gills are gray, light yellow, or even light purple. Its waxy hollow stem is bright yellow when young, aging into a dull brown or orange. Yellowfoot mushrooms grow in huge groups, with sometimes thousands of fruiting bodies appearing at the same time in moist, swampy areas.

HOW TO SPOT

Size: 0.8 to 2.8 inches (2 to 7.1 cm) wide; 1.2 to 3.5 inches (3 to 9 cm) tall

Color: Brown, gray, and yellow

Habitat: Coniferous forests

Range: Northern North America

CAULIFLOWER *(SPARASSIS CRISPA)*

The cauliflower mushroom gets its name from its unique wavy shape and its creamy white color. It makes its home in tree roots. If it lives on dead roots, it is saprotrophic, but if it takes over living roots, it is parasitic, although it doesn't harm the tree. An antifungal property helps it keep other kinds of fungi away. Cauliflowers can sometimes weigh as much as 50 pounds (22.7 kg). Considered highly edible, young cauliflowers have a sweet and earthy flavor.

HOW TO SPOT

Size: 7.9 to 15.7 inches (20 to 39.9 cm) wide

Color: White, tan

Habitat: Coniferous forests

Range: Western North America

DYER'S POLYPORE

(PHAEOLUS SCHWEINITZII)

Also known as the cowpie or velvet-top, this fungus enters trees through the tree's roots, causing these roots to decay. Eventually, the tree base weakens and the whole tree falls over. Young Dyer's polypores come in bright colors ranging from yellow to orange with a greenish pore surface. The top is velvety and the flesh is thin. Over time, the whole fungus becomes dark brown with a hard, brittle texture. Spores are spread by the wind, not from root to root.

HOW TO SPOT

Size: 5 to 10 inches (12.7 to 25.4 cm) wide

Color: Yellow, orange, brown

Habitat: Coniferous forests

Range: Across North America

FUN FACT

Dyer's polypore is a butt rot fungus. It attacks the butt of the tree, which is the thickest part of the tree above the root where the tree makes contact with the soil.

HEN-OF-THE-WOODS

(GRIFOLA FRONDOSA)

Also known as the maitake or the sheepshead mushrooms, hen-of-the-woods are a favorite of fall foragers. They grow near the base of trees and resemble a roosting chicken. Its brown or light-gray rosette-shaped caps are layered and grow out of a single stem. Pores underneath the caps are white but bruise brown if mishandled. Some specimens can grow up to 30 pounds (13.6 kg) in size. Larger trees grow larger mushrooms, and they grow back every year.

HOW TO SPOT

Size: 6 to 15.7 inches (15.2 to 39.9 cm) wide; 4 to 11.8 inches (10.2 to 30 cm) tall

Color: Brown or light gray

Habitat: Deciduous forests

Range: East of the Rocky Mountains

FUN FACT

Hen-of-the-woods can grow anywhere oaks are, including yards, parks, and golf courses.

HONEY *(ARMILLARIA MELLEA)*

Also known as the shoestring or bootlace, this fungus has thin, black fibers that stretch underground. They twist around tree roots, attacking and eventually killing the trees. It also attacks garden plants. The fruiting bodies appear in the late summer and grow in tightly packed clumps around the tree's base or stump. The mushroom's cap is sticky and freckled with dark brown scales. The gills underneath are lighter in color and can release millions of spores.

FUN FACT

The huge honey mushroom mycelium in Oregon is potentially the largest single organism in the world. Most of the year, it looks like a white layer that grows between tree bark and wood.

HOW TO SPOT

Size: 2 to 5 inches (5 to 12.7 cm) wide; 2.8 to 7.9 inches (7.1 to 20 cm) tall

Color: Yellow or brown

Habitat: Deciduous and coniferous forests

Range: Eastern half of the United States

LION'S MANE *(HERICIUM ERINACEUS)*

Lion's mane grows straight out of hardwood trees and forms a large pom-pom shape of long, dangling spines. However, young specimens appear as a single clump and do not develop spines until later. They attach high on dead and wounded hardwoods via a thick, spongy core. Lion's mane likes cooler weather and can be found in the fall and into winter. They grow alone or in pairs.

HOW TO SPOT

Size: 3.1 to 9.4 inches (7.9 to 23.9 cm) wide
Color: White
Habitat: Deciduous forests
Range: Throughout North America

MUSHROOM MEDS

Lion's mane is edible, with a seafood-like flavor. It is valued for its use in East Asian medicine. Research shows the mushroom does offer some health benefits, but it should not be a replacement for medical care.

LOBSTER *(HYPOMYCES LACTIFLUORUM)*

The lobster mushroom is a parasite to other mushrooms. *H. lactifluorum* covers *Russula* and *Lactarius* species with a bright fruiting body called perithecia, replacing the host's DNA with its own. By the time the lobster mushroom is fully grown, there is very little of the original host mushroom left. Fully formed lobsters are red or orange on the outside and white on the inside. There are no pores or gills. Lobsters are edible, with a seafood-like flavor.

HOW TO SPOT

Size: 6 to 8 inches (15.2 to 20.3 cm) tall

Color: Orange

Habitat: Deciduous and coniferous forests

Range: Throughout North America

REISHI *(GANODERMA OREGONENSE)*

Reishi mushrooms are valued in Asia for their medicinal properties. They only grow on wood, choosing decaying logs and stumps as well as wounded living trees. Their woody, cork-like texture makes them durable enough to last through cold winters. Caps are red or brown and shaped like kidneys or fans, although their host can play a role in their overall shape. Those growing on trees become more bracket-like, while mushrooms sprouting from a log often grow stems to help them grow outward from the log.

HOW TO SPOT

Size: 4 to 19.7 inches (10.2 to 50 cm) wide

Color: Red or brown

Habitat: Coniferous forests

Range: Western United States

PICKY PICKY

Sixteen varieties of reishi grow in North America. They are all very similar, and some can only be sorted with specific location information and DNA analysis. Usually, a species grows on either deciduous or coniferous trees, not both. Some are even pickier, growing on only one or two specific tree species.

WITCH'S BUTTER

(TREMELLA MESENTERICA)

Witch's butter is a parasite of another fungus. *Peniophora* is a type of crust fungus that forms on bark-covered hardwoods. But under the tree's bark, its mycelium can fall victim to witch's butter. Witch's butter feeds on and slowly covers the crust fungus with its own yellow, gelatinous fruiting body. Its lobes are moist and gelatinous, and although it looks soft, it has a tougher, more rubbery texture. In dry conditions, it shrinks and turns a darker orange but rehydrates when it rains.

HOW TO SPOT

Size: 1 to 3 inches (2.5 to 7.6 cm) wide; 1.3 to 1.6 inches (3.3 to 4.1 cm) tall

Color: Yellow

Habitat: Deciduous forests

Range: Across North America

A CRUSTY BUNCH

Crust fungi have smooth fruiting bodies that grow on any kind of wood. Because they are not edible, they are not well-studied. There could be as many as 1,300 different species in North America alone. Most are flat and crust-like, but some, such as witch's butter, are lumpy, while others grow as brackets.

ANGEL WING

(PLEUROCYBELLA PORRIGENS)

Angel wings are visually similar to oyster mushrooms. Their white, fluted caps are both trumpet-shaped and narrow at the base, with gills along the outside. They both grow on dead trees. Upon closer inspection, angel wings differ slightly. They grow more upright, like wings, and have thinner flesh. Angel wings grow only on conifers, while oysters are more common on deciduous hardwoods. They grow in overlapping clusters and can be found in the late fall.

HOW TO SPOT

Size: 1 to 4 inches (2.5 to 10.2 cm) wide
Color: White
Habitat: Coniferous forests
Range: Across North America

EDIBLE ENEMIES

Until the mid-2000s, field guides labeled angel wings as an edible variety of oyster mushroom. Then, in 2004, 59 people in Japan were poisoned after eating them, and 17 of those people died. It took as long as 31 days for symptoms to show up. Scientists are still not sure exactly what happened.

APRICOT JELLY

(GUEPINIA HELVELLOIDES)

Apricot jelly mushrooms are easy to recognize due to their unusual shape, color, and texture. They can withstand being dried and then rehydrated repeatedly. They produce spores each time they rehydrate. The fan-shaped, tongue-like cap is rolled at the edges and tapers into a stalk. Its underside is a paler shade of pink or apricot, fading to white as it nears the base. The flesh looks similar to jelly but feels more rubbery. It is considered edible, but not particularly delicious.

HOW TO SPOT

Size: 1 to 2.5 inches (2.5 to 6.4 cm) wide; 2 to 4 inches (5 to 10.2 cm) tall

Color: Salmon pink

Habitat: Coniferous forests

Range: Throughout North America

FUN FACT

Currently, *G. helvelloides* is the only mushroom in its genus.

ARTIST'S CONK

(GANODERMA APPLANATUM)

Artist's conk can be found year-round on dead or dying trees. These shelf mushrooms are both saprotrophic and parasitic, growing out of dead wood or in the wounds of living trees. They can live for more than a decade. When cut in half, each layer can be counted, much like tree rings. Their woody, firm cap is brown or gray on top and white on the bottom. When the porous undersurface is scratched with a sharp object, the cuts stain brown and stay that way once dried, which is what gives this mushroom its name.

HOW TO SPOT

Size: 4 to 20 inches (10.2 to 50.8 cm) wide

Color: Brown or gray cap, with white underside

Habitat: Deciduous forests

Range: Across North America

FUN FACT

Conk is a term for any kind of bracket or shelf fungi. These tough, sturdy fungi grow straight out of wood, like shelves. Their spores are produced on their undersides.

BEEFSTEAK *(FISTULINA HEPATICA)*

Beefsteaks are saprotrophic polypores but also slightly parasitic. They cause brown rot on living oak trees. They look like raw meat. Red liquid oozes out when the mushroom is cut or squeezed. The exterior is sticky or velvety to the touch. The inside is white and streaked with red. The underside is covered in light-colored pores that develop into tiny tubes. Each tube releases spores. This is one of the few mushrooms that can be eaten raw, but older specimens can taste sour or even cause stomach upset.

HOW TO SPOT

Size: 2.8 to 7.9 inches (7.1 to 20 cm) wide

Color: Red

Habitat: Deciduous forests

Range: Across North America, but more common east of the Rocky Mountains

FUN FACT

A polypore mushroom uses aboveground pores to release its spores, rather than gills or teeth.

BIRD'S NEST *(CRUCIBULUM LAEVE)*

A cup full of tiny "eggs" that grows out of wood debris, bird's nest fungi are easy to identify. They are small but tend to grow in large clusters. Young bird's nests are covered with a yellow, velvety membrane called an epiphragm that keeps rain out until the mushroom's "eggs," or peridioles, are fully grown. Each egg is filled with millions of spores and is attached to the cap with a thin, sticky cord called a funiculus. Falling raindrops launch the eggs up to 4 feet (1.2 m) away. The funiculus then sticks to plants and twigs.

HOW TO SPOT

Size: 0.2 to 0.4 inches (5 to 10.2 mm) wide; 0.1 to 0.4 inches (2.5 to 10.2 mm) tall

Color: Shades of yellow and brown

Habitat: Deciduous and coniferous forests

Range: Across North America

BITTER OYSTER *(PANELLUS STIPTICUS)*

These small mushrooms have a kidney-shaped cap fanning out of a short, tapering stem. The edges of the cap roll inward. Tightly packed gills fork and cross from the edge of the cap until abruptly ending at the stem. The bitter oyster is tough and velvety to the touch. It becomes wrinkled as it ages. Bioluminescence gives the bitter oyster a greenish-blue glow at night. Although bitter oyster grows across multiple continents, only strains in eastern North America glow. Scientists are still not sure why.

HOW TO SPOT

Size: 0.4 to 1.4 inches (1 to 3.6 cm) wide
Color: Light brown, tan
Habitat: Deciduous forests
Range: Across North America, but more common in the east

FUN FACT

Bitter oysters lose their bioluminescence when dried but glow again when rehydrated.

BLEWIT *(CLITOCYBE NUDA)*

Blewits start their lives in shades of lilac and purple but quickly fade to brown and buff. They can grow almost anywhere there is organic material, including compost, twigs, and grass clippings. Walkers often find patches of blewit along paths, as the mushroom prefers open areas. Blewits have a smooth cap that may look iridescent in sunlight. The stem is thicker at the bottom, and the gills are tightly packed. Blewits are edible, but older specimens can be confused with some poisonous *Cortinarius* varieties, so proceed with caution.

HOW TO SPOT

Size: 1.2 to 4.7 inches (3 to 11.9 cm) wide; 0.8 to 2.4 inches (2 to 6 cm) tall

Color: Purple, then tan

Habitat: Deciduous and coniferous forests

Range: Across North America

FUN FACT

Purple isn't the blewit's only bright color. Its spores are pale white or beige, but its spore print is pale pink!

BRAIN PUFFBALL

(CALVATIA CRANIIFORMIS)

The brain puffball grows along open, grassy areas. Young brain puffballs are white and round, with a firm, white interior, and show up in the summer. Over time, the shape changes to its signature brain shape as the mushroom grows over its base. The outside browns and gets cracked and wrinkly, revealing the now-powdery, yellowed spores inside. When touched by an animal, raindrops, or other outside forces, millions of spores are released into the air.

HOW TO SPOT

Size: 3.1 to 7.9 inches (7.9 to 20 cm) wide; 2.4 to 7.9 inches (6 to 20 cm) tall

Color: White or tan

Habitat: Deciduous forests and open ground

Range: Eastern and southern North America

BRICK CAP *(HYPHOLOMA LATERITIUM)*

The brick cap mushroom is a common growth on fallen hardwood. Young specimens have soft, cotton-like partial veils. The convex center of the cap is more pigmented, while the edges become paler along the outside. Remainders of the mushroom's veil may dot the edges and eventually disappear. Dark gray gills attach to the mushroom's slender stem that tapers near the bottom. Brick caps grow in large groups late in the fall, making them ideal for foragers.

HOW TO SPOT

Size: 1.2 to 3.9 inches (3 to 9.9 cm) wide; 1.6 to 4.7 inches (4 to 11.9 cm) tall

Color: Red, fading to buff

Habitat: Deciduous forests

Range: Across North America; most common in the northeast

CHICKEN OF THE WOODS

(LAETIPORUS SULPHUREUS)

Chicken of the woods has a soft, meaty texture. It is a food source around the world. Its bright orange color makes it easy to spot, and there are no look-alikes that pose a danger to beginner foragers. Both saprotrophic and parasitic, this mushroom grows on dead and living trees, causing brown rot or butt rot that kills the host. However, the host tree dies long before the fruiting body appears. *L. sulphureus* has white or off-white tubelike pores, while other varieties are more orange or pink.

HOW TO SPOT

Size: Up to 3 feet (0.9 m) wide

Color: Orange and peach

Habitat: Deciduous and coniferous forests

Range: East of the Rocky Mountains

FUN FACT

Bugs love chicken of the woods too! Shake out harvested mushrooms and then soak them in a mixture of one part vinegar to one part water to remove the bugs.

COLLARED EARTHSTAR

(GEASTRUM TRIPLEX)

The collared earthstar looks like something on the bottom of the sea. It first grows underground as mycelia. When it's time to reproduce, the fruiting body grows in the shape of a pointed bulb. The outer layer cracks, splitting into five to eight "arms" and revealing its spore sac. As the spores turn to powder, the outer layer of the sac dries and cracks. The arms dry up and shrink toward the center, pushing the sac higher and off the forest floor. After the spores are released, the dried outer layers remain behind.

HOW TO SPOT

Size: Up to 3.9 inches (9.9 cm) wide

Color: Brown and light brown

Habitat: Deciduous and coniferous forests

Range: United States east of the Mississippi River

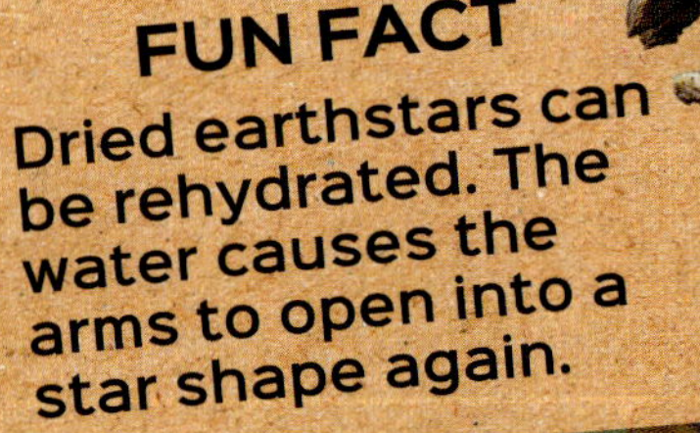

FUN FACT

Dried earthstars can be rehydrated. The water causes the arms to open into a star shape again.

COMB TOOTH *(HERICIUM CORALLOIDES)*

Comb tooth mushrooms, also known as coral tooth, grow out of dead wood as white branches covered in long rows of short, brittle spines up to 0.5 inches (1.3 cm) long. These mushrooms grow in the same place every year. They appear in the late summer and fall, producing spores in their spines. When young, the mushroom is white and edible, although it yellows and becomes bitter with age. Comb tooth mushrooms are believed to have medicinal properties.

HOW TO SPOT

Size: Up to 15.7 inches (39.9 cm) wide; 7.9 inches (20 cm) tall

Color: White

Habitat: Deciduous forests

Range: Across North America

COMMON BROWN CUP

(PEZIZA PHYLLOGENA)

Mushroom hunters often encounter the common brown cup while hunting for morels in the spring. These cup-shaped mushrooms come in shades of dark-, red-, or purple-brown and do not have a stem. Instead, they are attached to bark, logs, leaves, or another growing medium at a single point. The edges of the cap turn up and curl in when young but flatten as they age. Cell-sized spore sacs called asci contain eight spores apiece. When spores are ready, they burst out of the ascus.

HOW TO SPOT

Size: 1.2 to 5.9 inches (3 to 15 cm) wide

Color: Brown

Habitat: Deciduous and coniferous forests

Range: Across North America

COMMON CONECAP

(CONOCYBE TENERA)

The common conecap is small, plain, and easy to identify. Its small brown cap, which is usually no wider than 1 inch (2.5 cm), is cone-shaped when it's young and flattens out with age. The stalk is long and thin, made of brittle, fragile fibers. Gills are lighter than the cap but darken with age. The gills adnate, which means they are broadly attached to the stem rather than connecting closer to the top of the cap. Common conecaps grow in lawns, mulch, along the edge of woodlands, and other flat areas.

HOW TO SPOT

Size: 0.4 to 1.2 inches (1 to 3 cm) wide; 2 to 3.5 inches (5 to 8.9 cm) tall

Color: Light brown

Habitat: Flat, grassy areas

Range: Western North America

FUN FACT

The cap's conical shape gives this mushroom its other names: dunce cap or cone head.

COMMON PUFFBALL

(LYCOPERDON PERLATUM)

Many people see any sort of puffball mushroom and assume it's *L. perlatum*. However, this variety of mushroom has some distinguishing features. *L. perlatum's* spines are wide, cone-shaped, and turn brown at the tips. When removed, the spines leave a distinctive pockmark behind. The mushroom is curved or flared at the top, with a stem-like base. Young puffballs are white but age to brown or yellow. White puffballs are edible and can be found in the late spring through fall.

HOW TO SPOT

Size: 0.8 to 2.4 inches (2 to 6 cm) wide; 1.1 to 3.5 inches (2.8 to 8.9 cm) tall

Color: White

Habitat: Deciduous and coniferous forests; open, grassy areas

Range: Across North America

HOLD YOUR BREATH

People and animals who breathe in large amounts of puffball spores can get a rare but serious respiratory disease called lycoperdonosis. The spores are covered in tiny spines that can irritate the lungs. People who have asthma or allergies should be cautious and wear a mask when near these mushrooms.

COMMON STINKHORN

(PHALLUS IMPUDICUS)

The common stinkhorn is edible if you catch it early enough—the mushroom in its egg form is round and covered with a white, stretchy shell. The inside is crunchy and has been compared to a radish. But once it starts to "hatch," the smell of rotting meat or dung makes it much less appealing. The mushroom has an olive-colored, bell-shaped hat that oozes a spore-bearing gel called gleba, which is the cause of the odor. Insects are attracted to the gleba, spreading the spores around the forest. When the gleba is depleted, the hat turns white like the stem.

HOW TO SPOT

Size: Up to 9.8 inches (24.9 cm) tall

Color: White and brown

Habitat: Deciduous and coniferous forests

Range: Across North America; most common west of the Mississippi River

CROWN-TIPPED CORAL

(ARTOMYCES PYXIDATUS)

Although crown-tipped coral mushrooms have "coral" in the name, they are separate from regular coral mushrooms. Crown-tipped corals grow out of decaying wood. Each arm branches from a small, single point, not a large base. The connection point is white or light pink. Each fuzzy fruiting body has distinctive branches—and the branches may grow more branches. Lacking gills or pores, crown-tips grow their spores on the surface of the branches. The tips of the fruit have three to six small points around that form a "crown."

HOW TO SPOT

Size: 0.8 to 4 inches (2 to 10.2 cm) wide; 1.6 to 5.1 inches (4 to 13 cm) tall
Color: White, off-white, pink, yellow
Habitat: Deciduous forests
Range: East of the Rocky Mountains

LAND REEF

There are hundreds of coral, or clavaroid, mushrooms in the fungi family. Many *Ramaria* mushrooms are mistaken for crown-tips. However, *Ramarias* have more colorful fruiting bodies that grow out of the ground. Some branch like forks, and others look like worms or clubs.

DEAD MAN'S FINGER

(XYLARIA POLYMORPHA)

Young dead man's fingers appear in small groups as pale blue, club-shaped fruits with rounded white or off-white tips. The tip holds spores, which are released through a small hole. The inside of the fruiting body is white. As the mushroom ages, it turns a dull dark brown or black. The exterior dries out and becomes crusty. This fungus can infect fruit trees, causing them to grow a large crop of small fruit. Eventually, it can cause black root rot. By the time the fingers appear, the rot is serious.

HOW TO SPOT

Size: 0.4 to 1.2 inches (1 to 3 cm) wide; 1.6 to 5.5 inches (4 to 14 cm) tall

Color: Pale blue to black

Habitat: Deciduous forests

Range: East of the Rocky Mountains

DEAD MAN'S FINGERS ARE FOREVER

Dead man's fingers reproduce by making thread-like fingers called hyphae. The hyphae can live inside the host for a decade and can spread to new places if the host is moved or used as mulch. There is no way to kill dead man's fingers and no cure.

DEATH ANGEL *(AMANITA OCREATA)*

Unlike some of its more colorful *Amanita* relatives, the death angel is pale in comparison. Its creamy white, sometimes pinkish, cap is initially curved, eventually opening and even curving at the edges to reveal tightly packed white gills underneath. It has a white annulus ring near the top of the flared hollow stem. The stem, thicker than the stem of many other *Amanita* species, sits inside a white cup-shaped volva. One of the most toxic mushrooms in the world, death angels are not dangerous to touch but can cause severe organ failure if eaten.

HOW TO SPOT

Size: 2 to 5.1 inches (5 to 13 cm) wide; 3.9 to 8.7 inches (9.9 to 22 cm) tall

Color: White

Habitat: Deciduous and coniferous forests

Range: Western North America

FUN FACT

Death angels and death caps grow in the same area but in opposite seasons. *A. phalloides* grows in the fall and *A. ocreata* in the late winter and spring.

DEVIL'S CIGAR *(CHORIOACTIS GEASTER)*

Also known as the Texas star, the devil's cigar is the only species in the genus *Chorioactis*. It only grows in a handful of counties in northern Texas and Oklahoma and in a small area in Japan. In the late fall, a dark brown fruiting body resembling a cigar appears on decaying cedar elm stumps and roots. Later in the winter, the body hisses and releases spores into the sky. The fruiting body splits at the top, fanning out into a star shape with four to eight arms the color of leather.

HOW TO SPOT

Size: 3 to 4 inches (7.6 to 10.2 cm) tall

Color: Dark brown

Habitat: Deciduous forests

Range: Northern Texas and Oklahoma

FUN FACT

In 2021, *C. geaster* was named the official state mushroom of Texas. Minnesota, Oregon, California, and Utah are the only other states with a state mushroom.

DRYAD'S SADDLE

(CERIOPORUS SQUAMOSUS)

Dryad's saddle is both parasitic and saprotrophic. It grows on living and dead hardwood in the spring. On living trees, it causes white heart rot. It has a large fruiting body. Sometimes it grows alone, but other times there are many fruits that overlap and connect to a single velvety black base. The top is covered in round, brown scales that tend to resemble feathers. Over time, the brown fades to white or off-white. Underneath, tubes produce spores. The tubes are covered by pores, which release the spores.

HOW TO SPOT

Size: 3 to 18 inches (7.6 to 45.7 cm) wide

Color: Brown scales fading to white or off-white

Habitat: Deciduous forests

Range: Across North America

FUN FACT

Ancient Greek mythology imagined dryads as tree spirits or nymphs. They lived in trees and showed themselves to humans as beautiful women.

DUNG CANNON

(PILOBOLUS CRYSTALLINUS)

Dung cannons are saprotrophic, but not on trees like many mushrooms. Instead, they make their homes in poop. Found in the feces of herbivores, their life cycle sends them through the animal's digestive system. Spores are eaten, passed through the animal, and come out in manure. The fruiting body is a fluid-filled orb on top of a stalk. Using high pressure, it can launch its spores inside the orb into the air at 56 miles (90 km) per hour.

Size: Up to 2 inches (5 cm) tall
Color: Clear and jelly-like, with a black "hat"
Habitat: Grassy pastures
Range: Eastern and Midwest North America

FUN FACT

The black tip on top of the orbs contains the mushroom's spores. The spore sac launching through the air gives the mushroom its other common name: the hat thrower.

ELFIN SADDLE *(HELVELLA CRISPA)*

The elfin saddle has an unusual appearance, from its wrinkly, ribbed stem to its bumpy, saddle-shaped cap with irregular lobes. To reproduce, it shoots spores out the top of its cap. The underside is covered by a fine fuzz when young but smooths over time. The mushroom has a pleasant smell, but experts are not sure if it is edible. It may cause digestive upset and contain carcinogens.

FUN FACT

H. crispa may also be mycorrhizal. It grows on the ground as well as on hardwood trees.

HOW TO SPOT

Size: 0.8 to 2.4 inches (2 to 6 cm) wide; 1.2 to 5.1 inches (3 to 13 cm) tall

Color: White

Habitat: Deciduous forests

Range: Across North America

EYELASH CUP

(SCUTELLINIA SCUTELLATA)

This small cup mushroom grows in clusters on damp, rotting wood in the summer and fall. Young specimens have a shallow "cup" shape but flatten with age. Although they are small, they are one of the larger *Scutellinia* species. The fruiting bodies are bright red or orange. The edges are fringed with eyelash-like hairs that extend across the bottom of the cup. These stemless mushrooms attach directly to their host.

HOW TO SPOT

Size: Up to 0.4 inches (1 cm) wide
Color: Bright red or orange
Habitat: Deciduous and coniferous forests
Range: Across North America

FALSE MOREL *(GYROMITRA ESCULENTA)*

True morels are valued for their scarcity and their flavor. However, there are a number of look-alike species that can fool beginner foragers into thinking they've found the real thing. *G. esculenta* even means "edible" in Latin. But eating it can damage organs and the central nervous system. Looking closely at the cap can distinguish it from its tastier cousin. The false morel has rounded wrinkles, rather than tighter, pitted ridges. They are also not hollow all the way through. Instead, there are separate air pockets inside the cap.

HOW TO SPOT

Size: 0.8 to 2.8 inches (2 to 7.1 cm) wide

Color: Shades of brown or black; white to off-white stem

Habitat: Coniferous forests

Range: West of the Rocky Mountains

LOTS OF FAKERS

There are multiple mushroom species that are called false morels. They also have wrinkled caps and white stems. *Verpa conica* and *G. gigas* are two of them. Both are considered edible by some cultures, but they contain toxins that can affect people differently, especially if they are not prepared correctly.

FLUTED BIRD'S NEST

(CYATHUS STRIATUS)

The fluted bird's nest is shaped more like a deep cup. It typically grows on tree branches but is also found in mulch and wood chips. It can be easy to spot, as it often grows in large clusters. The outside of the cup is rough and bumpy, while the inside "cup" is grooved or fluted like a seashell and filled with small spore-containing capsules called peridioles. Raindrops send the peridioles flying up to 3 feet (0.9 m) into the air. A sticky exterior helps them grab onto wherever they land.

HOW TO SPOT

Size: 0.4 inches (1 cm) wide; 0.8 inches (2 cm) tall

Color: Dark on the outside; gray, white, or black inside

Habitat: Deciduous and coniferous forests

Range: Across North America

GIANT PUFFBALL *(CALVATIA GIGANTEA)*

At their largest, most puffball species grow to be around the size of a soccer ball. But the largest giant puffball ever recorded was more than 8 feet (2.4 m) across and weighed 48 pounds (21.8 kg). Giant puffballs begin appearing in the late summer, growing in areas of fallen leaves or in grass litter. When young, the whole mushroom is firm, white, and edible, but as the spores reach maturity, the interior turns powdery and a yellow-green color.

HOW TO SPOT

Size: 12 inches (30.5 cm) wide or larger
Color: White
Habitat: Deciduous forests
Range: East of the Rocky Mountains

FUN FACT

Giant puffballs release several trillion spores at a time, but they need perfect conditions to grow. Very few of the spores may actually result in another full-sized mushroom.

JACK-O-LANTERN

(OMPHALOTUS ILLUDENS)

The jack-o-lantern is beautiful to look at. It is also toxic to eat, although usually not deadly. Beginner foragers may confuse this toxic species with the chanterelle, especially as both grow in late summer to early fall. However, there are several differences. *O. illudens* grows in dense clusters and on both trees and the ground. It also has straight, narrow true gills that attach lower on the stalk, which is curved. The flattish, funnel-shaped cap has a dip near its center.

HOW TO SPOT

Size: 2 to 8 inches (5 to 20.3 cm) wide; 2 to 8 inches (5 to 20.3 cm) tall

Color: Orange

Habitat: Deciduous forests

Range: East of the Rocky Mountains

FUN FACT

Jack-o-lanterns are bioluminescent. Their gills glow green in the dark.

LITTLE PING PONG BAT

(PANELLUS PUSILLUS)

A small, wide, fan-shaped mushroom that grows out of logs in tiered clusters, the little ping pong bat almost looks as though it could be used for a game of table tennis. The top of the mushroom is creamy white, smooth, and convex. Large pores cover the bottom, and the stem attachment on the bottom is visible. The caps grow in large groups straight out from the stem and overlap each other. At night, the mushrooms can be seen glowing thanks to bioluminescence.

HOW TO SPOT

Size: 0.1 to 0.2 inches (0.3 to 0.5 cm) wide

Color: White

Habitat: Deciduous forests

Range: United States and Mexico

FUN FACT

The light from glowing fungi is also called foxfire. Scientists believe the glow is meant to attract insects, which help spread spores.

MICA CAP

(COPRINELLUS MICACEUS)

Mica caps grow in tight clusters near stumps or logs. Young specimens have oval-shaped caps that slump to a bell- or convex-shape as they age. The loose gills attach to the stem and eventually dissolve. Sparkly, mica-like granules that can be found on young mica caps gave the mushroom its name. Its thick stem is white or off-white, and while it looks sturdy, the inside is completely hollow. This edible mushroom must be eaten fairly quickly or the caps will liquify.

HOW TO SPOT

Size: 0.5 to 2 inches (1.3 to 5 cm) wide; 1 to 3 inches (2.5 to 7.6 cm) tall
Color: Light brown or amber
Habitat: Deciduous forests
Range: Across North America

A MUSHROOMY MEAL

The stage of liquifying is also known as deliquescence. Once a *Coprinellus* mushroom has released its spores, it begins consuming itself with its own enzymes. Its life cycle is over, and it quickly decomposes. It can take just a few hours for a mushroom to go from firm and edible to liquid goo.

MOREL *(MORCHELLA ESCULENTA)*

The common morel's tall, thin, honeycombed cap looks like a sponge. It is a rare, happy sight to mushroom hunters. Its bold, nutty flavor is highly sought after. Morels only grow a few weeks out of the year in places with extreme winter-to-summer changes. They have a sclerotium. This mass of hardened mycelium stores nutrients. During good growing periods, the sclerotium grows more mycelium. Only during perfect conditions does it produce fruiting bodies.

HOW TO SPOT

Size: 2.5 to 6 inches (6.4 to 15.2 cm) tall
Color: Light brown to brown cap; pale stem
Habitat: Coniferous forests
Range: Across North America

FUN FACT

While delicious when cooked, morels are toxic if eaten raw or undercooked.

OAK MAZEGILL *(DAEDALEA QUERCINA)*

The oak mazegill lives on oak trees and its gills are thick and mazelike, with branches that split multiple times. These polypores lack a stem and grow directly off hardwood trees singularly or in joined tiers. They come in a variety of sizes but can grow to be up to 3.1 inches (7.9 cm) thick. When young, it appears white or gray, but as it ages, it changes color to more closely resemble the oak tree's bark. The oak mazegill is not edible, with a hard, cork-like, brittle texture.

HOW TO SPOT

Size: Up to 8 inches (20.3 cm) wide

Color: White or gray turning reddish

Habitat: Deciduous forests

Range: Across North America, but rare west of the Mississippi

FUN FACT

The genus *Daedalea* is named after the Greek mythology character Daedalus, who designed the legendary labyrinth for King Minos.

OCTOPUS STINKHORN

(CLATHRUS ARCHERI)

In the late summer and early autumn, the fruiting body of an octopus stinkhorn sprouts from moist, shady, flat areas. Its young form appears as an egg-like sac. At this point, the fungus is edible. When its spores are ready, the fungal network emerges from the egg, reaching into the air before curling back down like octopus arms. Each of the fungus's four to eight arms are covered in dark red gleba that resembles blood and smells like rotting meat.

HOW TO SPOT

Size: Up to 6 inches (15.2 cm) tall
Color: White in egg form, then red
Habitat: Flat areas
Range: Northern California

ORANGE PEEL *(ALEURIA AURANTIA)*

Orange peel mushrooms grow in large clumps. The caps, initially cup-shaped, develop wavy edges. The inside of the cap is bright orange, while the underside is more matte and covered in a whitish fuzz. Although it has a thin flesh, its texture is brittle and leatherlike, which means it does not bruise but is more difficult to harvest. Unlike most mushrooms, the orange peel's spores are on the top of the cap. When mature, the spores shoot straight up into the air.

Size: Up to 4 inches (10.2 cm) wide; 0.8 to 1.6 inches (2 to 4 cm) tall
Color: Orange
Habitat: Flat areas
Range: Across North America

FUN FACT

The mushroom's vivid color is caused by carotenoids, especially beta-carotene. This also gives carrots, squash, and peppers their color.

OYSTER *(PLEUROTUS OSTREATUS)*

Oyster mushrooms are a common sight in the forest as well as at farmer's markets and grocery stores. Large and meaty, they grow in overlapping clusters, which makes gathering enough for a meal an easy task. The underside of the oyster-shaped cap is covered with decurrent gills. This means they are attached to the cap and run down most of the stem. Some oysters do not have a stem.

HOW TO SPOT

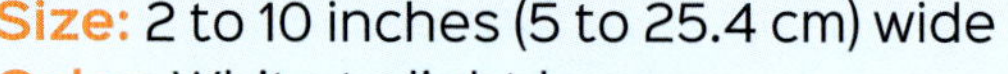
Size: 2 to 10 inches (5 to 25.4 cm) wide
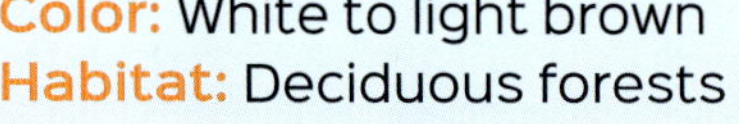
Color: White to light brown
Habitat: Deciduous forests
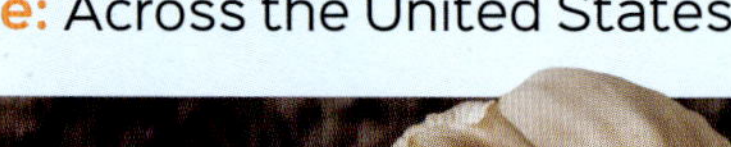
Range: Across the United States

FUN FACT

P. ostreatus is also known as the pearl oyster. But there are 201 other varieties of *Pleurotus* mushrooms, and all of them are edible.

WHO'S EATING WHOM?

Oyster mushrooms are carnivorous. They paralyze microscopic roundworms called nematodes with a toxin. Then, the mushroom's filament-like hyphae consume the nematode by breaking down its body and absorbing its nitrogen-rich nutrients.

PARASOL *(MACROLEPIOTA PROCERA)*

The parasol mushroom gets its name from its tall, skinny stem and wide cap. Its wide cap is egg-shaped, with a knob in the center. The stem is darker brown and scaly, with a ring near the middle. It is a popular edible mushroom, although it is often confused with the toxic green-spored lepiota. An easy way to tell them apart is by taking a spore print. Parasols leave a white or pale print. Lepiotas leave a green print.

Look-alikes aren't the only way mushrooms can be confused. Different mushrooms with similar names, such as false parasols and shaggy parasols, can cause confusion too!

HOW TO SPOT

Size: 3 to 8 inches (7.6 to 20.3 cm) wide; 5 to 16 inches (12.7 to 40.6 cm) tall

Color: White, buff, brown

Habitat: Grassy and flat areas

Range: Across North America

PORCINI *(BOLETUS EDULIS)*

Most people know *B. edulis* by one of its common names: porcini. It's also known as the penny bun or king bolete. When young, the cap is white, but as it ages, it turns brown and looks like a crusty dinner roll. Its thick stem has a net-like texture. Porcinis grow near tree roots, storing water and nutrients for the trees. Porcinis are full of amino acids called glutamates that give them an intense umami flavor.

HOW TO SPOT

Size: Up to 11.8 inches (30 cm) wide; 4 to 8 inches (10.2 to 20.3 cm) tall

Color: White and brown

Habitat: Deciduous and coniferous forests

Range: Across North America

FUN FACT

In Latin, *boletus* means "mushroom" and *edulis* means "edible."

PORTOBELLO *(AGARICUS BISPORUS)*

This fungus is found both in the wild and in grocery stores. White button mushrooms, brown cremini, and large portobellos are all *A. bisporus* at different levels of maturity. Portobellos need a nutrient-rich substrate to grow. The spores are easy to propagate by farmers and can be grown in humid, cool places such as caves, tunnels, and special warehouses. White mushrooms have a round cap and a closed veil. As the mushroom ages, the cap opens and turns brown. Fully grown portobellos have completely flat caps and exposed gills.

HOW TO SPOT

Size: 1 to 5.5 inches (2.5 to 14 cm) wide; 0.8 to 2.8 inches (2 to 7.1 cm) tall

Color: White and brown

Habitat: Grasslands and other flat areas

Range: Across North America

TASTY TREATS

Portobellos are a popular alternative to meat. Growing them is better for the environment than raising animals. One acre (0.4 ha) of land can produce a million pounds (453,592 kg) of mushrooms annually. About $1 billion of mushrooms are grown every year. Young white mushrooms are the most popular.

PRINCE AGARICUS

(AGARICUS AUGUSTUS)

Although they grow near coniferous trees, this mushroom usually appears along roadways or in parks rather than deep in the forest. The cap is large, covered with yellowish-brown scales. It starts in a box or cup shape but then becomes bumpy and convex. When bruised, the cap turns yellow or orange. It is one of the largest of its species, reaching sizes of up to 1 foot (0.3 m) across and 1 pound (0.5 kg). This mushroom smells like sweet almonds and has a similar taste.

HOW TO SPOT

Size: 2.4 to 12.6 inches (6 to 32 cm) wide; 4 to 14.6 inches (10.2 to 37 cm) tall

Color: White to yellow-brown

Habitat: Near coniferous trees

Range: Western North America

PURPLE JELLYDISC

(ASCOCORYNE SARCOIDES)

Growing in pink or purple clumps that resemble cups, discs, or even brains, the purple jellydisc fungus is a unique member of the fungi family. When young, it grows in a club shape, but later the lobes widen into discs or cups. They may have a small stem. This fungus produces spores and also reproduces asexually. The underside may feel fuzzy, while the flesh is gelatinous, odorless, and not considered edible.

HOW TO SPOT

Size: Up to 8 inches (20.3 cm) wide
Color: Purple or pink
Habitat: Deciduous forests
Range: Throughout North America

SLIME MOLDS

Slime molds are similar to jelly fungus. Once, scientists grouped the two together. But they are actually not part of the fungus family at all. These single-celled organisms are part of the amoeba family and have both plant and animal properties. Slime molds form when individual cells fuse together into one big mass.

RED BASKET STINKHORN

(CLATHRUS RUBER)

The red basket stinkhorn is also known as the red cage fungus, basket stinkhorn, and lattice stinkhorn. It appears in gardens, mulch, and the remains of woody plants. At first, it appears as small, white, or greenish eggs that attach to the ground by threads. They "hatch" when the fungus inside bursts up and forms a geometric cage. A smelly green slime attracts insects, which then fly away with the stinkhorn's spores attached. After a day or two, the fungus shrivels and disappears.

HOW TO SPOT

Size: 1.6 to 4 inches (4 to 10.2 cm) wide; 2 to 7 inches (5 to 17.8 cm) tall

Color: Bright red, pink, or orange

Habitat: Deciduous and coniferous forests

Range: Across the United States

RED BELTED CONK

(FOMITOPSIS MOUNCEAE)

The red belted conk appears on decaying logs in cooler areas. It can withstand very cold weather. The fungus causes brown rot on dead and dying trees, aiding in creating beneficial soil for the forest. Identifiable by thick red-and-orange bands edged with white, they can be observed year-round. Every year, a new layer of pores is added to the conk's cap. Some of the largest specimens can reach 18 inches (45.7 cm) wide and 7 inches (17.8 cm) thick.

HOW TO SPOT

Size: 3 to 10 inches (7.6 to 25.4 cm) wide
Color: Red, orange, and white
Habitat: Coniferous and deciduous forests
Range: Northern United States

LOST CONTRIBUTIONS

F. mounceae was named for mycologist Irene Mounce (1894–1989). She studied mushrooms for 25 years. Her career ended when she married in 1945, as at the time only unmarried women were allowed to have full-time jobs with the Canadian Department of Agriculture. This policy remained in place for a decade afterward.

SCARLET ELF CUP

(SARCOSCYPHA COCCINEA)

The scarlet elf cup grows on sticks and branches on the forest floor, appearing in the fall through the spring. Tiny stems blend into the fruiting body, especially as the fungus ages and the cup deepens. The inside of the cup is brightly colored, while the outside is pale and fuzzy, whitening with age. When scarlet elf cups are ready to reproduce, they shoot thousands of spores straight up with a puff of air.

HOW TO SPOT

Size: Up to 0.6 to 2 inches (1.5 to 5 cm) wide; 0.4 to 0.8 inches (1 to 2 cm) tall

Color: Bright red or orange

Habitat: Deciduous forests

Range: Northwestern United States

SHAGGY MANE *(COPRINUS COMATUS)*

In the summer and fall, shaggy manes grow out of disturbed earth as individuals, clusters, or fairy rings. Their tall, thin stems have a loose ring around them and are topped with cylinder-shaped young caps and bell-shaped older mushrooms. Both are covered in distinctive shaggy brown scales. When the mushrooms reach full maturity, the gills deliquesce, making the edges of the cap "drip" black ink. It is also known as the shaggy ink cap and the lawyer's wig.

HOW TO SPOT

Size: 1.2 to 5.9 inches (3 to 15 cm) wide; 2 to 7.9 inches (5 to 20 cm) tall

Color: White

Habitat: Flat areas of disturbed earth

Range: Northern North America

FUN FACT

Shaggy manes come in a variety of sizes. Huge specimens more than 1.6 feet (0.5 m) tall have been reported.

SHAGGY PARASOL

(CHLOROPHYLLUM RHACODES)

Young shaggy parasols have round caps on long stems that bulge at the bottom, which gives them their common name in Italy: the drum stick. They grow in freshly disturbed ground and in coniferous forests. Parasol mushrooms are highly edible and enjoyed by foragers, but their similarities to the green-spored lepiota adds a challenge. Shaggy parasols have a white spore print and flesh that bruises a pink-orange color. Its cap is shaggier as well.

HOW TO SPOT

Size: 2 to 6.3 inches (5 to 16 cm) wide; 2.4 to 8.3 inches (6 to 21 cm) tall
Color: White and brown
Habitat: Flat areas, coniferous forests
Range: East of the Rocky Mountains

SHIITAKE *(LENTINULA EDODES)*

The shiitake is native to East Asia but is the second-most cultivated mushroom in the world. Although it does not naturally appear in the wild, specimens have been found along the East Coast of the United States. With all the farmed spores, it seems likely that some would escape and find the perfect home. It has an umbrella-shaped cap and a thin, curved stem. Gills are white or cream underneath.

HOW TO SPOT

Size: 3 to 6 inches (7.6 to 15.2 cm) wide; 2 to 4 inches (5 to 10.2 cm) tall
Color: Light brown
Habitat: Deciduous forests
Range: East Coast of United States

FUN FACT

Valued for its meaty flavor, shiitakes are also used by some to treat diseases such as AIDS, cancer, heart disease, and diabetes.

NO MUSHROOMS FOR YOU

Until the 1970s, growing or importing shiitakes in the United States was banned because it was confused with its cousin, *Neolentius lepideus*. It is called the train wrecker mushroom. It grows on train ties and causes the treated lumber to rot faster. However, it is much less delicious.

SPLITGILL *(SCHIZOPHYLLUM COMMUNE)*

The stemless splitgill attaches itself directly to dead wood the way bracket fungi do. Unlike a true bracket, this mushroom does not have tube-like pores. Its gills fold against themselves with a divide down the middle. The split allows the fungus to dry out and rehydrate—or close and re-open—multiple times during its lifespan. They can stay dry for years before getting water again. The gills also split when it is time to release spores.

HOW TO SPOT

Size: 0.4 to 1.6 inches (1 to 4 cm) wide

Color: White or gray

Habitat: Deciduous forests

Range: Across North America

FUN FACT

The splitgill is the most common and farthest-reaching mushroom on Earth. It can be found on every continent except Antarctica.

STRAW *(VOLVARIELLA VOLVACEA)*

A non-native species, the straw is grown in Southeast Asia as an important food source. It made its way to North America through mulch, compost, and wood chips. It thrives during hot summers, fruiting above 80 degrees Fahrenheit (27 degrees Celsius). They appear as clusters of blackish eggs that quickly fruit in less than a week. Fully grown straw mushrooms are grayish-brown with fine visible fibers. The dense gills are white or pink and do not attach to the stem, which has a thick volva.

HOW TO SPOT

Size: 2 to 4.7 inches (5 to 11.9 cm) wide; 2.4 to 4.7 inches (6 to 11.9 cm) tall

Color: Dark gray to white

Habitat: Flat areas, gardens, compost

Range: Across North America

FUN FACT

These mushrooms do not last long, especially when refrigerated. They are commonly sold canned or dried.

SUN *(AGARICUS SUBRUFESCENS)*

Many countries value the "mushroom of the sun" for its medicinal properties. A cousin of the portobello, it was first grown as a crop in the late 1800s and is now grown and sold around the world. It has a light brown cap and white flesh. Gills are tightly packed and brownish-pink. The stem is white, with a soft partial veil and a ring around its middle.

HOW TO SPOT

Size: 2.4 to 5.2 inches (6 to 13.2 cm) wide
Color: Light brown
Habitat: Flat, open areas
Range: Northeast North America

FUN FACT

Its strong almond-like smell gives the sun mushroom its other nickname, the almond agaricus.

TURKEY TAIL *(TRAMETES VERSICOLOR)*

One of the most common mushrooms in North America, the turkey tail grows anywhere there is dead wood. This bracket grows in layers of color, showing off stripes of browns, grays, reds, and blues. It always has a margin of white along the edge. The underside is porous and there is no stem. Turkey tails grow in overlapping rows or in rosettes. Their flesh is tough, velvety on the outside and rubbery on the inside.

HOW TO SPOT

Size: 0.8 to 3.1 inches (2 to 7.9 cm) wide
Color: Various shades of brown
Habitat: Deciduous and coniferous forests
Range: Across North America

FUN FACT

The turkey tail has a look-alike, *Stereum ostrea*. However, *S. ostrea* is a crust fungus, not a bracket. Its underside is smooth, rather than porous.

VEILED LADY STINKHORN

(PHALLUS INDUSIATUS)

Veiled lady stinkhorns, also known as bridal veils, begin as small pale pink or white eggs. Inside the egg is the stinkhorn stalk covered in gelatinous goo. The egg "hatches" to reveal a plain white stalk. The mushroom's dark cap expands, decorated with a lacy white skirt that's nearly as long as its stalk. The mushroom's smelly gleba attracts insects, who distribute the mushroom's spores.

HOW TO SPOT

Size: 1.6 inches (4 cm) wide; up to 7.9 inches (20 cm) tall
Color: White
Habitat: Rainforests
Range: Mexico

VIOLET-TOOTHED POLYPORE

(TRICHAPTUM BIFORME)

Violet-toothed polypores look like a faded version of its relative, the turkey tail. The top of the curved bracket mushroom is layered shades of sandy brown and trimmed in light purple. But the porous, toothy underside hides the big flash of color, a rainbow of deeper purples and lilacs, although the color fades as the mushroom ages. The cap is tough, woody, and covered in hair. Violet-toothed polypores grow in dense, overlapping clusters.

HOW TO SPOT

Size: Up to 3 inches (7.6 cm) wide
Color: Light browns, purples
Habitat: Deciduous forests
Range: Across North America

FUN FACT

Violet-toothed polypores can be found in all 50 states and are the most commonly encountered wild fungus in eastern North America.

VOMITING RUSSULA

(RUSSULA EMETICA)

With a nickname like the Sickener, there is no question that eating the vomiting russula would be a bad idea. Its bright red cap peels slightly along the edges, beginning as a cap and flattening to a flatter vase shape. The broad, closely packed gills underneath attach to the flared off-white stalk and crumble easily. Five *Russula* species share the same range, and none are safe to eat. *R. emetica* is the easiest to identify by its spicy flavor.

HOW TO SPOT

Size: 1.2 to 3.9 inches (3 to 9.9 cm) wide; 1.6 to 4 inches (4 to 10.2 cm) tall
Color: Red and white
Habitat: Coniferous forests
Range: Northern North America

FUN FACT

Emetica is a Greek word that describes something that causes vomiting.

WEEPING WILLOW

(LACRYMARIA LACRYMABUNDA)

Young weeping willows are bell-shaped and covered in a thick layer of wool. The furry veil clings to the mushroom as it ages. The cap flattens but usually retains a hump in the middle. Gills are initially light brown but then darken with spores. When the mushroom gets wet, the edges of the gills turn water droplets black, making it appear that the whole mushroom is crying. Weeping willows make fruit in mid-summer through the fall.

HOW TO SPOT

Size: 1.6 to 4.7 inches (4 to 11.9 cm) wide; 2 to 3.9 inches (5 to 9.9 cm) tall

Color: Light brown

Habitat: Flat, open areas

Range: Across North America

WOOD EAR *(AURICULARIA AMERICANA)*

The wood ear is also known as the jelly ear because of its rubbery, jelly-like texture. It appears after rain or in damp areas. Young wood ears have a dusting of white and fine fuzz. They grow in many different shapes, including cups, fans, and ears, but no matter what the shape, they are always wavy and grouped together. Wood ears can dry out and rehydrate many times and appear in every season except winter.

FUN FACT

Wood ears do not have much flavor, but they have a crunchy, seaweed-like texture. They are often used in soups and stir-fries.

HOW TO SPOT

Size: 0.8 to 2 inches (2 to 5 cm) wide
Color: Reddish brown
Habitat: Deciduous or coniferous trees
Range: Across North America

WRINKLED PEACH

(RHODOTUS PALMATUS)

The wrinkled peach, also known as the rosy veincap, grows out of freshly felled trees such as elm, maple, and basswood. The pink wrinkled cap is attached to a small, curved stem and can range in colors depending on the light wavelengths it is exposed to during development. The thick gills are white or pale peach, attaching to the ringless stem. Wrinkled peaches may weep red or orange liquid if they grow too quickly.

HOW TO SPOT

Size: 1.2 to 3.1 inches (3 to 7.9 cm) wide; 0.4 to 1.6 inches (1 to 4 cm) tall

Color: Pink, orange-yellow

Habitat: Deciduous forests

Range: Northeast North America

FUN FACT

There are only two members in the *Rhodotus* genus. The other, *R. asperior*, is only found in China.

SEASONS AND WRINKLES

During spring and summer, the mushroom develops deep wrinkles and a pale peach color. During the fall, it grows fewer wrinkles and takes on a more orange tone.

DEVIL'S MATCHSTICK

(PILOPHORUS ACICULARIS)

This lichen's shape makes it look like a match—or a nail, which is how it gets its other common name, nail lichen. The fungus's primary body grows as thin white crust that covers the ground. Its secondary body contains the straight, stick-like shapes that grow together in clumps. Each stick is topped with a black ball, which contains the fruiting body and spores. Foragers often find devil's matchstick in cool, moist forests, especially near waterfalls.

HOW TO SPOT

Size: 0.2 to 1.2 inches (0.5 to 3 cm) tall
Color: Greenish white, black
Habitat: Deciduous and coniferous forests
Range: Northwestern United States

FUN FACT

There are at least 13,000 different lichen species around the world. But scientists think that there could be two, or even three, times that number just waiting to be discovered.

WHAT'S THE LIFE OF A LICHEN LIKE?

Lichens are a symbiotic partnership between fungi and algae or cyanobacteria. The fungi's hyphae provide the lichen's main structure. The algae use photosynthesis to make food that it shares with the fungi. Map lichen is the oldest lichen in the world. Some specimens are believed to be more than 8,600 years old.

OLD MAN'S BEARD

(USNEA LONGISSIMA)

Most lichen can be found on the ground. But other species take root in the trees. Members of the *Usnea* genus hang off tree branches. There is a central cord with shorter, even branches hanging from it. The main cord does not have an outer layer, which gives it a soft snow-white appearance, while the branches have a green exterior layer. The lichen grows on coniferous trees near bodies of water. To reproduce, pieces of the lichen break off, and the wind carries them to new places. This is called fragmentation.

HOW TO SPOT

Size: Main cord 6 inches (15.2 cm) to 20 feet (6.1 m) long; branches 2 to 2.8 inches (5 to 7.1 cm) long

Color: Yellow-green

Habitat: Coniferous forests

Range: Across North America

LOSING THE BEARD

Old man's beard was once found across the United States, from the Pacific Coast, along the Great Lakes, and down the Atlantic Coast. However, habitat loss and pollution have made this lichen a rare find. It is sensitive to pollution, and toxic chemicals can stop the lichen from completing its reproductive cycles.

REINDEER MOSS

(CLADONIA RANGIFERINA)

Reindeer moss is common throughout the Arctic, serving as a food source for reindeer, moose, musk ox, caribou, and other grazing animals. Birds also use it to build nests. Although it does not grow fast—at around 0.1 to 0.2 inches (0.3 to 0.5 cm) per year—it covers wide stretches of the ground. Reindeer moss absorbs water and minerals and plays a big role in preventing soil erosion and ensuring the health of its ecosystem.

FUN FACT

Reindeer moss can live for more than 100 years! However, this means that damage can take a long time to repair.

HOW TO SPOT

Size: Up to 3 inches (7.6 cm) tall
Color: Gray-white
Habitat: Deciduous forests
Range: Northern North America

TRUMPET CUP *(CLADONIA FIMBRIATA)*

The trumpet cup is widespread in Canada but has been spotted in mountain ranges as far south as Colorado and Kentucky. It thrives in the shade and in acidic soil. The tiny white or gray cups are covered in fine green soredia, which are the fungus's reproductive structures and are made up of both algae and fungi combined. The soredia are spread by wind or rain. Trumpet cups can be found on every continent except Antarctica.

HOW TO SPOT

Size: 0.2 inches (0.5 cm) wide; 0.2 to 0.6 inches (0.5 to 1.5 cm) tall

Color: White, gray, green

Habitat: Mossy areas

Range: Mainly Canada

FUN FACT

Lichens grow slowly. Some grow only 0.2 inches (0.5 cm) a year. But they can live for many years.

WITCH'S HAIR *(ALECTORIA SARMENTOSA)*

Witch's hair hangs off trees in moist, old-growth forests. It gets its color from its algae, while the fungal body protects it and feeds it food and water. Hyphae keep the lichen from being completely limp and from blowing away. The fungus reproduces asexually by breaking off parts of its body and letting them catch the wind. It also reproduces sexually by growing small, brown, cup-shaped mushrooms that release spores. However, sexual reproduction only spreads the fungi, not the algae.

HOW TO SPOT

Size: 7.9 to 15.7 inches (20 to 39.9 cm) long

Color: Greenish gray

Habitat: Coniferous forests and deciduous shrubs

Range: Across North America

FUN FACT

Old man's beard has a central stem, but witch's hair does not. Witch's hair is a large mass of strands tangled together.

WOLF LICHEN *(LETHARIA VULPINA)*

Most lichens get their color from their algae. Wolf lichen's bright green color, however, comes from its poisonous vulpinic acid. Long ago, it was ground up and used to poison wolves and foxes. It can also keep harmful garden pests, such as slugs and snails, away from fruits and vegetables. *L. vulpine* reproduces asexually, releasing small pieces of itself that can germinate in a new location.

HOW TO SPOT

Size: 1.2 to 3.1 inches (3 to 7.9 cm) wide
Color: Bright green
Habitat: Coniferous forests
Range: Western North America

FUN FACT

Vulpinic acid is toxic if eaten and can also be absorbed through the skin.

CORN SMUT *(USTILAGO MAYDIS)*

Corn smut is a biotroph. It creates a parasitic relationship with its host without killing it. *U. maydis* spores enter the corn through the tasseled silk and make their way down the ear, turning even, golden kernels into lumpy, gray tumors called galls in as fast as a day. The galls continue to grow until they burst, releasing black spores into the air. *U. maydis* naturally occurs in soil and can move in wind and water.

HOW TO SPOT

Size: N/A
Color: Gray
Habitat: Corn and maize fields
Range: Across North America

FUN FACT

Most farmers consider corn smut destructive, spending millions of dollars to get rid of "devil's corn." But others enjoy the taste. In Mexico, it is called *huitlacoche* and is valued for its flavorful, truffle-like flavor.

STINKING SMUT *(TILLETIA TRITICI)*

T. tritici is known as stinking smut or stinking bunt because of its fishy odor. The fungus infects the protective barrier around grass seedlings, planting its mycelia into the plant's tissues. The mycelia take over the plant's reproductive tissues. Instead of wheat kernels, the plant grows dull gray bunt balls. Each ball is full of spores that infect the surrounding soil. When the wheat is harvested, the bunt balls mix in with healthy seeds, which allow the spores to spread into additional crops.

HOW TO SPOT

Size: N/A
Color: Dark brown or black
Habitat: Wheat and wild grass fields
Range: Across North America

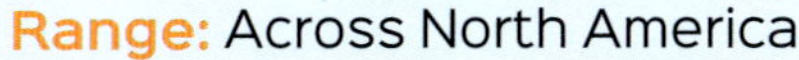

FUN FACT

Smut and bunts are plant diseases caused by fungi that affect grasses such as wheat, sugarcane, and corn. Parasitic fungi infect the host plant and produce spores in the plant's seeds.

BLACK STEM RUST

(PUCCINIA GRAMINIS)

Rusts are fungal diseases. Black stem rust infects cereal crops such as wheat, rye, oats, and barley, as well as barberry and wild grasses and grains. Reddish-brown spore masses cover the plant's stem and leaves, causing them to turn yellow and affecting the grain or seeds. Eventually, the spores turn black. Strong breezes allow the fungus to jump from one host to another. It is also spread by people. Its yellow spores are visible on shoes and clothing.

HOW TO SPOT

Size: N/A
Color: Red
Habitat: Grasses and cereal crop fields
Range: Northern and Midwestern United States

ERGOT *(CLAVICEPS PURPUREA)*

Ergot infects cereal plants such as wheat, barley, and rye, as well as some wild grasses. It takes over the plant's reproductive systems and replaces them with its own mycelium. Instead of kernels, the plants grow large seed-like fungal bodies called sclerotia. Eventually, the sclerotia drop off and spend the winter on the ground. In the spring, they germinate and spread once again. Consuming ergot can be harmful or even fatal to animals, including humans.

HOW TO SPOT

Size: Up to 0.8 inches (2 cm) long
Color: Purple-black
Habitat: Grasses and cereal crops
Range: Northern plains of North America

FUN FACT

Consuming ergot, especially ergot growing on rye, can cause a bacterial infection called St. Anthony's Fire. Patients feel an intense burning pain on their face and legs.

HOLLYHOCK RUST

(PUCCINIA MALVACEARUM)

Despite its name, hollyhock rust also affects ornamental plants and weeds in the mallow family. It spreads quickly, stunting the plant's growth or even killing it. Starting as orange or yellow spots on the plant's leaves, it progresses to brown or dark bumps along the leaves' undersides. Eventually, it creates holes in the leaves, which causes them to shrivel or die. The rust uses the wind, rain, or other water sources to spread its spores.

FUN FACT

Mallows are one of the most popular ornamental plants. The common mallow grows in the wild, although because it is not native to North America, it can be considered invasive.

HOW TO SPOT

Size: 0.05 to 0.1 inches (0.1 to 0.3 cm) in diameter
Color: Orange-yellow
Habitat: Gardens, lawns, and other flat areas
Range: Across North America

SCARLET CATERPILLARCLUB

(CORDYCEPS MILITARIS)

Sometimes butterfly or moth larvae do not make it to adulthood. Instead, they are attacked by *C. militaris*. The fungus mummifies the larva by filling it with its own mycelium. The larva's body becomes nourishment for the mushroom's fruiting body, which grows out of the larva's head and body. The fungus then sends its spores into the air, continuing its life cycle. *C. militaris* isn't edible when raw, but it has been used in medicine to treat various diseases.

HOW TO SPOT

Size: 0.8 to 3.1 inches (2 to 7.9 cm)
Color: Orange or red
Habitat: Deciduous and coniferous forests
Range: Across North America

FUN FACT

Some insects can sense when one has been infected by *Cordyceps*. They kill that individual and remove its body before the parasite can spore.

WHITE PINE BLISTER RUST

(CRONARTIUM RIBICOLA)

White pine blister rust was brought to North America around 1900 and spread quickly. The mycelium infects the white pine tree's needles. In the spring, it travels along the tree's needles to its branches, creating dead sections of bark called cankers that appear as yellow blisters. Eventually, the cankers form all the way around the tree, killing it. Spores burst from the cankers, spreading to infect a secondary host. Spores that form on that secondary host infect more white pines.

FUN FACT

Many rusts need a secondary, unrelated host to complete their life cycle. *C. ribicola* infects woody shrubs called ribes, which include gooseberries and currants.

HOW TO SPOT

Size: N/A
Color: Yellow-orange
Habitat: Coniferous forests
Range: Across northern North America

ZOMBIE-ANT FUNGUS

(OPHIOCORDYCEPS UNILATERALIS SENSU LATO)

Until 2014, scientists didn't think the zombie-ant fungus existed in the United States. But then, specimens were discovered in South Carolina. This fungus targets ants and spiders. Victims leave the safety of their tree canopy and walk like zombies, staggering and falling down. Then, they bite down on a leaf or stem and stay there until death. A few days later, the fruiting body of the fungus sprouts out of the ant's head. Other worker ants pick up the fungus spores and continue the cycle.

HOW TO SPOT

Size: N/A
Color: Red-brown
Habitat: Tropical forests
Range: South Carolina

FUN FACT

***Cordyceps* prefer temperatures between 77 and 86 degrees Fahrenheit (25 and 30 degrees Celsius). Human bodies are around 98 degrees F (36.7 degrees C).**

WHAT'S IN A NAME?

Ophiocordyceps unilateralis sensu lato is the fungus's temporary scientific name. *Sensu lato* means "in the broad sense," which tells scientists that it is recognized as a subspecies but does not yet have its own official name. More research must be done to figure out whether the North American variety is the same as the variety found in tropical forests.

GLOSSARY

annulus
A ring-like structure sometimes found on the stem, or stipe, of a mushroom.

coniferous
Referring to cone-bearing trees or shrubs with needle-shaped leaves.

deciduous
Referring to a tree or shrub that sheds its leaves annually.

forager
A person who searches for food in the wild.

gill
The papery rib under a mushroom's cap.

hypha
A fungus's long, branching thread.

invasive
Something that spreads and takes over an environment.

mycelium
A fungus's main mass made up of hyphae.

photosynthesis
The process that organisms use to turn sunlight into food.

spore
The reproductive gene of a fungus.

symbiotic
Referring to a beneficial relationship between two living things.

umami
A taste sensation that is savory and meaty.

veil
The thin membrane that covers the cap and stalk of a young mushroom.

volva
A sack of tissue that remains at the base of the stem.

TO LEARN MORE

FURTHER READINGS

Boddy, Lynne. *Humongous Fungus*. DK Publishing, 2021.

Debbink, Andrea. *Trees*. Abdo Reference, an imprint of Abdo Publishing, 2021.

Owen, Ruth. *Creepy Crawly Slime Molds*. Ruby Tuesday Books, 2021.

ONLINE RESOURCES

To learn more about mushrooms and other fungi, please visit **abdobooklinks.com** or scan this QR code. These links are routinely monitored and updated to provide the most current information available.

PHOTO CREDITS

Cover Photos: Jolanda Aalbers/Shutterstock, front (collared earthstar); David Clapp/Stone/Getty Images, front (fly amanita); Frost79/Shutterstock, front (trumpet cup); John Navajo/Shutterstock, front (wrinkled peach); thatmacroguy/Shutterstock, front (vomiting russula); bob.leccinum. Robert Kozak/Shutterstock, front (splitgill), front (bitter oyster); Photort/Shutterstock, front (Dyer's polypore); vitals/Shutterstock, front (chanterelle); Protasov AN/Shutterstock, front (hollyhock rust); Barry Blackburn/Shutterstock, front (American slender Caesar); godi photo/Shutterstock, front (amethyst deceiver); Gertjan Hooijer/Shutterstock, back (orange peel); HHelene/Shutterstock, back (yellowfoot) Interior Photos: HHelene/Shutterstock, 1 (top left), 29 (bottom); Tintila Corina/Shutterstock, 1 (top center), 10 (right), 27 (bottom), 44 (top); bogdan ionescu/Shutterstock, 1 (top right), 14 (bottom), 27 (top), 55 (bottom); John Navajo/Shutterstock, 1 (bottom left), 28 (bottom), 93 (bottom); Svitlyk/Shutterstock, 1 (bottom right), 43 (bottom), 106 (top); ewaplesna/Shutterstock, 4 (top right), 68 (top right); ANUCHA PALAMA/Shutterstock, 4 (bottom left), 90 (top left); JulieAlexK/iStock/Getty Images, 4 (bottom center), 83 (top); David Osborn/Shutterstock, 4 (bottom right), 48 (top); Kaiskynet Studio/Shutterstock, 5 (top left), 85 (bottom left); Gajda/Shutterstock, 5 (top center), 21 (bottom); vitals/Shutterstock, 5 (top right), 12 (bottom), 32 (top); KPiv/Shutterstock, 5 (bottom left); 8 (top); 8 (bottom); godi photo/Shutterstock, 9, 52 (right), 70 (top left); Sarah2/Shutterstock, 10 (left); Henri Koskinen/Shutterstock, 11 (top), 12 (top), 28 (top), 69 (top); Lorenzo Martinelli/Shutterstock, 11 (bottom); TimoH/Shutterstock, 13; Bukhta Yurii/Shutterstock, 14 (top); igor.kramar. shots/Shutterstock, 15; K Quinn Ferris/Dreamstime.com, 16; nickkurzenko/iStock/Getty Images, 17 (top), 19 (top center); Virginia Zabaleta/Shutterstock, 17 (bottom); David Clapp/Stone/Getty Images, 18 (top); Nikolay 007/Shutterstock, 18 (bottom); Lingkon Serao/Shutterstock, 19 (top right); Supratchai Pimpaeng/Shutterstock, 19 (bottom left); muuraa/Shutterstock, 20 (top); Adrian_am13/Shutterstock, 20 (bottom), 74 (top), 77 (top); Mykes Logos (MykesLogos)/Mushroom Observer/Wikimedia Commons, 21 (top); Matt Pulk/iNaturalist, 22; The Register-Guard/AP Images, 23 (left); John Loo/Flickr, 23 (right); A.S.Floro/Shutterstock, 24 (top), 63 (top); OVKNHR/Shutterstock, 24 (bottom); yevgeniy11/Shutterstock, 25 (top), 112 (center); Machacekcz/iStock/Getty Images, 25 (bottom), 44 (bottom); Krzycho/Shutterstock, 26; dabjola/Shutterstock, 29 (top); petratrollgrafik/Shutterstock, 30 (top); Jaroslav Machacek/Shutterstock, 30 (bottom); Photort/Shutterstock, 31 (top), 31 (bottom); Gertjan Hooijer/Shutterstock, 32 (bottom), 70 (top right), 71 (bottom); Zbigniew Dziok/Shutterstock, 33 (top); Southern Wind/Shutterstock, 33 (bottom); Karel Bock/Shutterstock, 34 (left); IgorCheri/Shutterstock, 34 (right); Kimberly Boyles/Shutterstock, 35 (top); James Mahan/iStock/Getty Images, 35 (bottom); Kathleen Dobson/iNaturalist, 36 (left), 36 (right); samray/Shutterstock, 37 (left); DreMac/Shutterstock, 37 (right); Wayward_hiker1/Shutterstock, 38 (right); Maria Dryfhout/Shutterstock, 38 (center); Gerald Corsi/iStock/Getty Images, 39 (top); Angela Ma/Forest Service Alaska Region, USDA/Flickr, 39 (bottom); Wieland Teixeira/Shutterstock, 40 (top); svf74/Shutterstock, 40 (bottom); Jolanda Aalbers/Shutterstock, 41 (top), 48 (bottom), 60 (bottom), 77 (bottom); Digoarpi/Shutterstock, 41 (bottom); NK-55/Shutterstock, 42 (top), 91 (top); Gilles San Martin/Flickr, 42 (bottom); Arterra/Universal Images Group/Getty Images, 43 (top), 64 (bottom), 97 (bottom); WIRACHAIPHOTO/Shutterstock, 45; PATSTOCK/Moment/Getty Images, 46; Marc Venema/Shutterstock, 47 (top); Pi-Lens/Shutterstock, 47 (bottom); weinkoetz/Shutterstock, 49 (top); Karl Ander Adami/iStock/Getty Images, 49 (bottom);

Paul Starosta/Stone/Getty Images, 50 (top); Maple Ferryman/Shutterstock, 50 (bottom); Sigur/Shutterstock, 51 (top); DragicaP/Shutterstock, 51 (bottom); Ivan Marjanovic/Shutterstock, 52 (left); Tomasz Czadowski/Shutterstock, 53 (top), 73 (right), 112 (right); iwciagr/Shutterstock, 53 (bottom), 61 (bottom); Muhammed Zeynel Ozturk/iStock/Getty Images, 54 (left); Igor Kramar/iStock/Getty Images, 54 (right); Rejdan/Shutterstock, 55 (top); Didier Veillon/iStock/Getty Images, 56 (top); J. Maughn/Flickr, 56 (bottom); RainbowHummingbird/iNaturalist, 57 (top); Gregg M. Pasterick/Shutterstock, 57 (bottom); SBWorldphotography/iStock/Getty Images, 58 (top); AndyScott/Wikimedia Commons, 58 (bottom), 112 (left); Sava Krstic (sava)/Mushroom Observer/Wikimedia Commons, 59 (top), 59 (bottom); Svetlana Mahovskaya/Shutterstock, 60 (top); melody.dyui/Shutterstock, 61 (top); Saaster/iStock/Getty Images, 62 (top); Ksenia Lada/Shutterstock, 62 (bottom); RATCHANAT BUA-NGERN/Shutterstock, 63 (bottom); Ugorenkov Aleksandr/Shutterstock, 64 (top); Kagenmi/iStock/Getty Images, 65 (top); Judy M Darby/Shutterstock, 65 (bottom); Reiner Richter/iNaturalist, 66 (top); Alison Harrington/Flickr, 66 (bottom); Wirestock/iStock/Getty Images, 67; TYNZA/Shutterstock, 68 (top left); AleksandarMilutinovic/Shutterstock, 68 (bottom), 78 (top), 80 (bottom); Björn S.../Flickr, 69 (bottom); Dusan Matousek/Shutterstock, 70 (bottom); J Need/Shutterstock, 71 (top); shaftinaction/Shutterstock, 72; Ninevija/Shutterstock, 73 (left); Adam J/Shutterstock, 74 (bottom); barmalini/Shutterstock, 75 (top middle); SweetLemons/Shutterstock, 75 (bottom left); misszin/Shutterstock, 75 (bottom right); dabjola/iStock/Getty Images, 76; PolyakovaN/Shutterstock, 78 (bottom); Robin Mulvey/Forest Health Protection, Forest Service, USDA, Alaska Region/Flickr, 79; Ivan Protsiuk/Shutterstock, 80 (top); CarlosR/Shutterstock, 81 (top); Gerrit Lammers/Shutterstock, 81 (bottom); Tom Meaker/iStock/Getty Images, 82 (top); Stephan Morris/Shutterstock, 82 (bottom); Gray wagtail/Shutterstock, 83 (bottom); Anne Powell/Shutterstock, 84 (top); Iva Vagnerova/iStock/Getty Images, 84 (bottom); Hans Maverric Jailin/Shutterstock, 85 (top); Banditta Art/Shutterstock, 85 (bottom right); Doso Winarno/Shutterstock, 86 (top); Picture Partners/Shutterstock, 86 (bottom); Jennifer Gauld/Shutterstock, 87; Jamikorn Sooktaramorn/Shutterstock, 88 (top); I Wayan Sumatika/Shutterstock, 88 (bottom); Urmas Ojango/Flickr, 89 (top), 89 (bottom); thatmacroguy/Shutterstock, 90 (top right); Alan Tunnicliffe/Shutterstock, 90 (bottom); weinkoetz/iStock/Getty Images, 91 (bottom); CampSmoke/Shutterstock, 92 (top); Noah Siegel/USDA Forest Service/Mushroom Observer/Wikimedia Commons, 92 (bottom); Arie v.d. Wolde/Shutterstock, 93 (top); YiBaoTY/iStock/Getty Images, 94 (top); Tab Tannery/Flickr, 94 (bottom); John Game/Flickr, 95 (top); Federica Grassi/Moment/Getty Images, 95 (bottom); ANGHI/Shutterstock, 96 (top); AleksandrN/Shutterstock, 96 (bottom); Janny2/Shutterstock, 97 (top); Awana JF/Shutterstock, 98 (top); SF photo/Shutterstock, 98 (bottom); Gerry Bishop/Shutterstock, 99 (top); Katja Schulz/Flickr, 99 (bottom); Belish/Shutterstock, 100 (top); Emilio100/Shutterstock, 100 (bottom); Tomasz Klejdysz/iStock/Getty Images, 101 (top), 101 (bottom); Damian Herde/Shutterstock, 102 (top); Yue Jin/USDA Agricultural Research Service, 102 (bottom); Manfred Ruckszio/Shutterstock, 103 (top); emer1940/iStock/Getty Images, 103 (bottom); Protasov AN/Shutterstock, 104 (left), 104 (right); bob.leccinum.Robert Kozak/Shutterstock, 105; Tomasz Klejdysz/Shutterstock, 106 (bottom), Reza Saputra/iStock/Getty Images, 107 (top); Vinicius R. Souza/Shutterstock, 107 (bottom)

ABDOBOOKS.COM
Published by Abdo Reference, a division of ABDO, PO Box 398166, Minneapolis, Minnesota 55439.

Printed in China.
102024
012025

Editor: Jane Katirgis
Series Designer: Colleen McLaren

Library of Congress Control Number: 2024938355
Publisher's Cataloging-in-Publication Data
Names: Bolte, Mari, author.
Title: Mushrooms and other fungi / by Mari Bolte
Description: Minneapolis, Minnesota : Abdo Reference, 2025 | Series: North American field guides | Includes online resources and index.
Identifiers: ISBN 9781098296155 (lib. bdg.) | ISBN 9798384917151 (ebook)
Subjects: LCSH: Mushrooms--Juvenile literature. | Mushrooms--Identification--Juvenile literature. | Fungi--Juvenile literature. | Fungi--Ecology--Juvenile literature. | Ecological science--Juvenile literature.
Classification: DDC 589.2--dc23